I WILL Bless Thee

I0167613

McDougal & Associates

Servants of Christ and Stewards of the
Mysteries of God

I WILL Bless Thee

Discovering the Untapped Power of COVENANT

by

David Harewood

All Scripture references are from the
Authorized King James Version of the Bible.

I WILL BLESS THEE
Copyright © 2011—David Harewood
ALL RIGHTS RESERVED!

No part of this book may be reproduced or transmitted in any form
or by any means, electronic or mechanical, including photocopying,
recording, or by any information retrieval system.

Published by:

McDougal & Associates
18896 Greenwell Springs RD
Greenwell Springs, LA 70739-0194
www.thepublishedword.com

McDougal & Associates is dedicated to the spreading of the
Gospel of Jesus Christ to as many people as possible in the
shortest time possible.

ISBN 978-1-934769-15-7

Printed on demand in the US, the UK and Australia
For Worldwide Distribution

Now the LORD had said unto Abram,

Get thee out of thy country, and from thy kindred, and from thy father's house, unto a land that I will shew thee:
And I will make of thee a great nation,
And I WILL BLESS THEE, and make thy name great;
And thou shalt be a blessing:
And I will bless them that bless thee, and curse him that curseth thee:
And in thee shall all families of the earth be blessed.

Genesis 12:1-3

COVENANT:

"An agreement, usually formal, between two or more persons to do or not do something specified."

Dictionary.com

"A solemn agreement to engage in or refrain from a specified action. It is commonly found in religious contexts, where it refers to sacred agreements between God and human beings."

Wikipedia

CONTENTS

INTRODUCTION

We are at one of the greatest moments of Church history, and to miss God at this time would be to miss Him forever. If you miss a bus, you can often catch another one, but there is something so important about this particular moment in time for the Church. Don't miss out on what God is doing right now.

It is time for the Church to rise up in power and become the beacon God intended it to be, and to my way of thinking, one of the most important reason we have not yet done this is that we have failed to understand the concept of covenant and, in particular, God's personal covenant with each of us, and therefore, we have left the provisions of our covenant largely untapped. If we don't know what we have, how can we use it or use it effectively?

There are many questions about covenant that are answered in this book. For instance:

- What exactly is a covenant?
- What are the promises of covenant?
- What are the responsibilities of covenant?
- What is the process of covenant?
- What did the covenant that God forged with men of old mean to them and what, if anything, does it mean to us today?

- What is the personal covenant God wants to make with YOU?
- How does covenant affect families?
- How are God's covenant and His love linked?
- Why is love the accepted identifier for all true believers in Christ?
- Is it right to make a covenant with other people today?
- If so, how do we know how to seek the right kind of agreement and avoid the wrong kind of agreement?

It is my prayer that you may find this message enlightening and life-changing and that through it, you may find yourself *Discovering the Untapped Power of Covenant.*

Apostle David Harewood
Baton Rouge, Louisiana

Part I

THE FOUNDATIONS OF COVENANT

Chapter 1

WHAT EXACTLY IS A COVENANT?

Now the LORD had said unto Abram, Get thee out of thy country, and from thy kindred, and from thy father's house, unto a land that I will shew thee: and I will make of thee a great nation, and I will bless thee, and make thy name great; and thou shalt be a blessing: and I will bless them that bless thee, and curse him that curseth thee: and in thee shall all families of the earth be blessed.   Genesis 12:1-3

God made a covenant with our forefather Abraham, the father of the faith, but what does that mean to us today? What exactly is a covenant anyway?

As noted in the front matter, a covenant is a legal agreement between two or more parties regarding a prescribed course of action. So why is our particular covenant, or formal agreement, so important? It's because it is a covenant forged with the Creator Himself. What could be more important than that?

If properly executed, a covenant is a legally binding contract. Can you imagine? We have a legal contract with the God of the Universe, and in that contract He has promised to bless and prosper us. It's all in writing, and it is sealed with the very blood of Jesus Christ. How exciting!

Before we get into the details of the power of our covenant, the security of it, the promise of it, the responsibility of it and the process of it, let's think first about covenants in general and what they mean.

A PARTNERSHIP AGREEMENT

There are many different types of covenants. There is, for instance, a covenant that is strictly a business matter. In this type of covenant, two business people or two separate businesses join hands with the hope of developing a larger market share. They thus strengthen each other by combining experiences and talents as well as physical assets. This is often called a partnership agreement, and the agreement defines what the responsibilities and potential earnings of each party will be during the effective period of the covenant. Human nature being what it is, such agreements must be protected by law, and either business party can later come back and make a legal demand on a party that does not live up to its contractual obligations.

There is also a clause in the agreement defining what will happen if this proves to be the case. The desire of both parties going into the agreement is good, to maintain the partnership healthy and viable, but if one or the other fails to fulfill his obligations, there are specific penalties.

A PRENUPTIAL AGREEMENT

Another type of covenant is called a prenuptial agreement. Such an agreement is entered into by a man and a woman hoping to spend the rest of their lives together but feeling that they must protect their assets in the event that their prospective spouse fails to live up to the agreement for any reason. Sadly, experience shows that it happens, so the use of such agreements is more and more common today.

Typically, a prenuptial agreement specifies exactly what assets a spouse agrees to give up the rights to in the event of the dissolution of the marriage by divorce or death. The very sad thing about such an agreement, drawn with the meticulous skill of an experienced lawyer and then signed by two parties, is that apparently the couple has already agreed to let their marriage fail at some point. Otherwise, why draw up such papers in the first place?

My question to any couple filing such papers is this: why get married in the first place if you plan to let the marriage fail when things get rough? Rather than trust in a prenuptial agreement, it would be better to trust in a marriage covenant (another type of binding contract) and work to make your marriage last. When God is in a thing, nothing can stop it, and it will prevail. But that is another subject for another book.

A TRADE AGREEMENT

Another common type of covenant is called a trade agreement. This is an agreement resulting from collective bargaining, often between nations. Two nations strike a deal with each other for future trade of goods and services. Not surprisingly, not every nation keeps its promises, and the aggrieved nation must then call into play clauses in the trade agreement requiring sanctions against the guilty party.

When mad cow disease appeared in American beef cattle, many countries broke their agreement to purchase American beef. In this case, they had a legitimate reason for breaking the covenant. Who wants to be even more crazy than they already are? In general, covenants are not to be broken and are protected by law so that they will not be broken.

Men, being men, break their covenants, but what we can say for sure is that God has never broken one of His many covenants with men, and because He is faithful, He expects us to be faithful to our part of the bargain as well.

THE VERY BEST AGREEMENT AVAILABLE

Of course, this book is not about trade agreements, prenuptial agreements, partnership agreements or any of the other types of earthly legally binding agreement. Rather, it's about something much more important: the covenant God wants to make with you personally. Such a covenant, if agreed upon by both parties, can change the course of your life and set you on the road to eternal life, physical health and financial prosperity. It can bless not only you individually, but also your entire family, your community and nation and even many generations to come.

The God of the Universe is ready to bless you. Will you agree with Him today and begin *Discovering the Untapped Power of Covenant?*

Chapter 2

THE POWER OF COVENANT

Behold, the days come, saith the LORD, that I will make a new covenant with the house of Israel, and with the house of Judah: not according to the covenant that I made with their fathers in the day that I took them by the hand to bring them out of the land of Egypt; which my covenant they brake, although I was an husband unto them, saith the LORD: but this shall be the covenant that I will make with the house of Israel; After those days, saith the LORD, I will put my law in their inward parts, and write it in their hearts; and will be their God, and they shall be my people. And they shall teach no more every man his neighbour, and every man his brother, saying, Know the LORD: for they shall all know me, from the least of them unto the greatest of them, saith the LORD: for I will forgive their iniquity, and I will remember their sin no more.

Jeremiah 31:31-34

The writer to the Hebrews also spoke of this covenant and in similar terms:

For if that first covenant had been faultless, then should no place have been sought for the second. For finding fault with them, he saith, Behold, the days come, saith the Lord, when I will make a new covenant with the house of Israel and with the house of Judah: not according to the covenant that I made with their fathers in the day when I took them by the hand to lead them out of the land of Egypt; because they continued not in my covenant, and I regarded them not, saith the Lord. For this is the covenant that I will make with the house of Israel after those days, saith the Lord; I will put my laws into their mind, and write them in their hearts: and I will be to them a God, and they shall be to me a people: and they shall not teach every man his neighbour, and every man his brother, saying, Know the Lord: for all shall know me, from the least to the greatest. Hebrews 8:7-11

The covenant Israel enjoyed during Old Testament times was glorious, but God had something even better in mind for us. The people of Israel enjoyed His protection from their enemies, His daily provision for themselves and their families (even in difficult times), and the assurance that they were the people of God (with all this meant). Now, God said, He would do a new thing. Instead of writing His laws on tables of stone (as He had done for Israel under Moses), He would write them in men's hearts and minds. This would result in something even more glorious for our time.

WHY GOD RAISED UP THE NATION OF ISRAEL

In ancient times, God raised up the Jewish people to show the world what a blessed nation would look like. While the rest of the nations were bowing down to images made of brick, stone and wood, God raised up a man and revealed Himself to that man.

Then, from that man, he formed an entire nation of believers, a peculiar people who would trust Him in all things and be faithful to Him in all things. He used this new nation (Israel) to reveal His precepts and principles to the whole world.

WE ALSO HAVE IDOLS

Today we scorn the idea of worshipping graven images, but our idols are just more sophisticated and modern. Here in America today, we actually worship cars and jobs, and we also worship people. An idol is just whatever takes the place of God in your life, and we have plenty of those.

Just as God called Abram out of the idolatry of his day, He calls us today to a higher life of knowing Him and being His people on the Earth. He extends to us the invitation to enter into sacred covenant with Him.

GOD REVEALS HIMSELF

While the ancient world was yet steeped in idolatry, God revealed Himself to Abraham as Jehovah. But, some would say, "That was then, and this is now. What of to-day?" The answer is that our God has not changed. As the Scriptures declare, He is the same *"yesterday, and to day and forever"* (Hebrews 13:8).

God's plan for His people today is no less glorious than for the ancient peoples. Rather than reveal Himself through a particular nation, He has now chosen to do it through the Church.

THE FORMATION OF THE CHURCH

In the course of time, God chose to reveal Himself in the form of human flesh, through a man who was called Jesus, and Jesus set about to build God's Church in the Earth. He said:

> *Upon this rock I will build my church; and the gates of hell shall not prevail against it.*   Matthew 16:18

Now, instead of one nation of people, God raised up a Church made up of believers from every nation under Heaven. Some of them *were* Jews, but many were Gentiles. To each of them, the Lord revealed Himself, and He promised: "If you are willing to believe on Jesus, My Son, trust in Him and commit your life to Him, I will make a covenant with you, and you will become a member of the Body of Christ on the Earth, which is the true Church, the *ecclesia* or body of called-out ones." Called to what?

CALLED TO WHAT?

We have been called to come out from a world of sin, perversion, degradation and everything that damned the human race. Just as Israel was called out of Egypt, God says to us today: "I brought you out with a strong hand, and have made you My people, the Church of the living God, the pillar and ground of all truth." Today we stand at a very serious threshold, knowing that Christ is about to come and take His Church out of this world. Because of that, He is working to perfect and strengthen the Church so that the gates of Hell cannot prevail against it, and He is using the Church to speak to the nations.

When God called Israel to be a peculiar nation among all the nations, He made a covenant with her, and, in the same way, He is making a covenant with us today, to bless us and reveal Himself through us to the nations in this final hour.

Once again, covenant is an agreement, usually formal and binding, between two or more persons to do or not do something specified. God has entered into such an agreement with you and with me, and He has promised to do many wonderful things for us. Now, it's up to us to fulfill our part of the bargain.

WHAT THE CHURCH IS ALL ABOUT

The Church is to be a model for all the nations. It is to reveal to all that Jesus Christ is Lord. This is important. Far too many still don't know what the Church is all about. For many, it is just a play thing, or a place where people gather on Sundays (and many of them worship a God they don't even know). But one of the principle laws of New Testament covenant with God is that we know Him. God said: *"They shall know me."*

The apostle Paul, after all of his wonderful experiences, cried out:

> *That I may know him, and the power of his resurrection, and the fellowship of his sufferings, being made conformable unto his death.* Philippians 3:10

"That I may know Him!" There could be no greater goal in life. Get to know who Jesus is. He is mighty to save and strong to deliver, and He is a covenant-keeping Lord. Unless you know Him, how can God use you to reveal His great love to others?

THE SERIOUSNESS OF OUR COVENANT

That first covenant made with the nation of Israel had weaknesses, but now it has been replaced with a new and better one, and we can all be partakers of it.

Our covenant is much more than a simple contract, although there are similarities. Both are intended to be binding agreements, but contracts are broken every day. This covenant, on the other hand, must never be broken.

In his book, *Up from Slavery*, the famous Booker T. Washington spoke of the power of covenant. He said he once met an ex-slave. Before the issuance of the Emancipation Proclamation, this man's owner announced to all his slaves that they could buy their freedom if they wanted and if they could. Hearing that better wages were being offered in Ohio, the man traveled there from Virginia (where he was living at the time) and took a job. Each payday he sent a good portion of his pay back to his master in Virginia. When Booker T. Washington met the man, he had just $300 left to pay for his freedom. But, in the meantime, the Emancipation Proclamation had been issued, and all slaves were freed. But, the man insisted, since he had the money, he would make the trip to Virginia to personally put the last payment in his master's hand.

"Why did he need to do that now?" everyone wondered. By law, he was a free man. But he insisted, "We had an agreement, and I can't break my word." That's the power of covenant.

DOING YOUR PART

This sacred agreement, or covenant, is between two parties: you and God. In covenant with you, God has promised to bless you, but you, in covenant with God, have made a promise to serve Him, to live for Him, to be obedient to Him. He has made a whole series of promises

to you, and your promise to Him is to love Him with all
your heart, with all your soul and with all your might.
And you also promise to love your neighbor as yourself.
God's promises fill the pages of the Bible, and yet even
it could not contain them all. He makes many unique
promises to you personally. What a wonderful thing this
covenant is!

That former slave kept his agreement and paid his
redemption money in full, and when he did, he felt that
something had been released in his life. He was not sorry
he had paid the money; he was glad.

Today, we treat promises far too lightly. We make
them today and break them tomorrow and think nothing
of it. Today, we say, "I love You Lord and commit everything to You," and tomorrow, by our attitude and actions,
we show that we don't trust God at all. God wants to do
something wonderful for us, but we have to take hold of
the covenant He offers and see that we do our part. The
many things the Old Covenant could not do are now possible, but we have to be willing to work with God and let
Him have His way in our lives so that these promises can
come to pass.

ARE YOU READY?

God is ready to make a new covenant with you. Are
you ready to let Him into your life? He wants you to become His chosen people on the Earth today. He wants
to use you to reveal to the nations who He is and what

He can do. He wants to make you an example to all those around you. He is offering you a new and better covenant. Are you willing to accept His offer fully and without reservation?

What God did for the nation of Israel was glorious, but what God will do today through His Church will be much more glorious. Will you be a part of that?

A COVENANT FOR PRAISERS

This new covenant is for *"the house of Judah,"* and Judah means praise. That's why our churches must be full of praise to God, and that's why the devil hates praise and praisers so much. He'll do anything to keep God's people from praising their mighty Creator.

Because of this, we must insist on living a life of praise. The man or woman who lives a life void of praise will be anemic, and, sad to say, there are a lot of those among us today. So much so that the Bible must declare:

> *We then that are strong ought to bear the infirmities of the weak, and not to please ourselves.*
>
> Romans 15:1

If you are weak today, don't stay that way. In God, you can be strong. Don't remain in your weakness for even one more hour or one more day. The covenant-keeping God extends His invitation to you today to live in a glorious new partnership with Him. What are you waiting on?

MUCH MORE GLORIOUS

Our new covenant is so much more glorious than the the covenant God made with Israel of old that it is not even to be compared. The Israelites were unable to keep their covenant with God, for it was based on the "thou shalt nots" of the Ten Commandments, and yet many today are attempting to live their lives in that same way:

> *Thou shalt not make unto thee any graven image.*
> Exodus 20:4

> *Thou shalt not bow down thyself to them.*
> Exodus 20:5

> *Thou shalt not take the name of the* Lord *thy God in vain.*
> Exodus 20:7

> *Thou shalt not kill.*   Exodus 20:13

> *Thou shalt not commit adultery.*   Exodus 20:14

> *Thou shalt not steal.*   Exodus 20:15

> *Thou shalt not bear false witness against thy neighbour.*
> Exodus 20:16

> *Thou shalt not covet thy neighbour's house, thou shalt not covet thy neighbour's wife, nor his manservant,*

nor his maidservant, nor his ox, nor his ass, nor any thing that is thy neighbour's. Exodus 20:17

If you can keep these commandments for two days, invariably you will break them on the third. The people of Israel couldn't keep them commandments, and you can't either (in your own strength).

The Israelites were lacking the most important of the commandments, and Jesus instituted it when He came to Earth, calling it *"a new commandment"*:

A new commandment I give unto you, That ye love one another; as I have loved you, that ye also love one another. John 13:34

This was more than a new commandment; it was a new covenant, God's covenant of love manifested to us and then through us to others. He loves you, and when you love Him, you can keep His commandments (by His strength in you). And then all men will know that you are His disciples because they will see His love demonstrated in and through you. (For more on this important subject of covenant love, see chapters 14-19).

WHY AND HOW DOES IT WORK?

Why does covenant work now when it didn't work before? And just how does it work? God said:

I will put my laws into their mind, and write them

in their hearts: and I will be to them a God, and they
shall be to me a people.   Hebrews 8:10

In other words, true covenant living changes your mind. If you are to be a proper representative of the Lord Jesus Christ on the Earth, your thinking must change. If you've heard that old expression, "It's a mind thing," then you know what I'm talking about. Our minds must be changed if we are to accomplish God's will here on this Earth.

You can't remain the person you grew up being. Through life experiences, your mind has been trained to assume certain things, and that has to change. God does things differently, and the natural mind is actually His enemy:

Because the carnal mind is enmity against God: for
it is not subject to the law of God, neither indeed can
be.   Romans 8:7

TAKING ON THE MIND OF CHRIST

Amazingly we are called upon to take unto us the very *"mind of Christ"*:

Let this mind be in you, which was also in Christ
Jesus.   Philippians 2:5

What was the mind of Christ like? We read on:

Who, being in the form of God, thought it not robbery to be equal with God: but made himself of no reputation, and took upon him the form of a servant, and was made in the likeness of men: and being found in fashion as a man, he humbled himself, and became obedient unto death, even the death of the cross.   Philippians 2:6-8

It was when Jesus humble Himself in this ways that Father God exalted Him:

Wherefore God also hath highly exalted him, and given him a name which is above every name: that at the name of Jesus every knee should bow, of things in heaven, and things in earth, and things under the earth; and that every tongue should confess that Jesus Christ is Lord, to the glory of God the Father.   Philippians 2:9-11

That's the mind we need if we are to make it as a real Christian in the midst of this wicked generation. God will write something in your mind that will make you able to overcome the temptations of this present world, and you will wake up in the morning thinking about it. As the hymn-writer said, "I woke up this morning with my mind stayed on Jesus."

Stayed on what? "Stayed on Jesus," not all the junk and filth that is around us.

MY FIRST THOUGHT EVERY MORNING

Every morning, the first thing I want to do is say, "Lord, thank You." That's not the result of brainwashing. It's because I've read and studied God's Word enough that its promises stick with me, and therefore Jesus is on my mind every single day.

This is the will of God for each of us. He wants to write His laws in our hearts and minds, and we desperately need Him to do that very thing.

THE CULMINATION OF THE PROMISE

The culmination of God's promise of covenant is this:

I will be to them a God ... .   Hebrews 8:10

God is the Creator, and He wants to become our personal Creator. God is the Deliverer, and He wants to become our personal Deliverer. God is the Sustainer, and He wants to become our personal Sustainer. God is the Provider, and He wants to become our personal Provider. God is the Healer, and He wants to become our personal Healer. God is the Baptizer, and He wants to become our personal Baptizer. All too often we look elsewhere for what we need, when the God of the Universe desires to become our personal God.

He is El-Shaddai, the many-breasted One, and He wants to become our personal El-Shaddai. He has what you need, and you can freely draw it from Him.

God is the Problem Solver, and He wants to become our personal Problem Solver.

God is the Heavy Load Bearer, and He wants to become our personal Heavy Load Bearer.

God can be and do all of this for you personally if you are willing for Him to come in and regulate your mind, placing His own thoughts in it. The result is that He will be your personal God.

GOD HAS DONE HIS PART

There is one more part of that verse. It goes on to say: "*And they shall be to me a people.*" God has done His part; now it's up to you to do yours.

Who is this "*they*" who will be "*a people*" to God? It is whosoever will. It is you, if you're willing. Because of this promise, you can declare, "I am a child of God. God loves me. God has made me His own. I am the person God has been looking for. I will be humble before Him. I will live my life to please Him." It's your choice, and if you make it, many wonderful things await you.

The result of such a decision, God showed us, will be glorious:

> *And they shall teach no more every man his neighbour, and every man his brother, saying, Know the LORD: for they shall all know me, from the least of them unto the greatest of them, saith the LORD.*
>
> Jeremiah 31:34

33

"They shall all know Me." That is one of the primary characteristics and primary requirements for this covenant-keeping people. *All* shall know Him.

UNDERSTANDING THE CONCEPT OF COVENANT IS IMPORTANT

Understanding the concept of covenant is important for every believer. If I fail to walk in covenant relationship with God, no one else can do it for me. I must make myself available to Him. Since the earliest times in the Garden of Eden, He has been searching for those who would believe and obey Him. Can you imagine a God who would humble Himself enough to come down and look for the creature He has formed? That's exactly what God did with Adam.

"Adam," He called, "where are you?" In the cool of the day each and every day He came to commune with His beloved creature, and He has not stopped doing that in this twenty-first century. If you have not enjoyed this type of personal fellowship with God it only means that you have not yet gotten yourself into the place that frees Him to come down and walk and talk with you. He wants to do it; that's for certain.

You may have missed Him because you're too busy doing everything else. If you'll just slow down a little, He'll be there for you.

WHAT'S OUR BIG HURRY?

That's right. Slow down, and let God manifest

His presence to you. Why is it that we have to pass everybody on the highway? Why is it that we don't have time even to greet people along the way? We're so busy, and we have so many important things to do and important places to go. But slowing down might save you from getting speeding tickets (I've never gotten one in my life), and it will also do a lot for your spiritual life.

Slow down. Leave a little earlier so that you can enjoy the journey. Take time to bow your head and give thanks to God before you gobble down your fast food. When you take time for the Creator, you'll find that He has time to answer you. His promise is:

> Behold, the LORD's hand is not shortened, that it cannot save; neither his ear heavy, that it cannot hear.
>
> Isaiah 59:1

When the smallest child calls upon Him, He hears them and responds. Take time to commune with Him today.

YOUR CHOICE

This is serious business. God will have Himself a people in this generation, and whether or not you are part of that people is your choice.

The people who respond to His call will then lighten the way and put forth an example for living, so that men and women everywhere can see His glorious light and be saved. So we have a great purpose, and that purpose is to be a light to the heathen of our generation.

WHO ARE THE HEATHEN OF OUR GENERATION?

Who are the heathen of our generation? They are those who don't go to God's house to honor Him; nor do they live for Him from day to day. This includes those who were once saved, but who decided, for some strange reason, that the world had more to offer them than God. So they turned their back on Him.

You and I are left standing, and it's up to us to show forth the goodness of Lord in our communities and our nations. This current generation must have a witness, and the Church the Lord Jesus Christ has built must stand firm. He declared that the gates of Hell would not prevail against us, and it must not.

WRITING THE LAST CHAPTER OF CHURCH HISTORY

We are in one of the greatest hours ever, and we will now write the last chapter of the history of the Church, but we cannot do it without a deep understanding of the power of our covenant with God. We cannot guess our way through the terrible trials to come. How will we do that?

Every time I enter the church in Baton Rouge, Louisiana, over which God has placed me as pastor, I feel God's power. This happens even when I am just driving by the place. It reminds me of the moment when Solomon took over the kingdom from his father David. The young Solomon made a very memorable speech that day. Among other things, he said that whenever the people were faced by any enemy if they would only focus their vision toward the holy Temple in Jerusalem, God would give them victory over their adversaries. This is true for any current need we might have as well. God demonstrates His power in and through the Church, and if we can focus on who He is there and what He does there, we can be delivered and healed. That's just how powerful our covenant with God is today.

God is writing His will in our hearts today, and it's for a divine purpose. Will you begin today *Discovering the Untapped Power of Covenant?*

Chapter 3

THE SECURITY OF COVENANT

And the word of the LORD came unto Jeremiah, saying, Thus saith the LORD; If ye can break my covenant of the day, and my covenant of the night, and that there should not be day and night in their season; then may also my covenant be broken with David my servant, that he should not have a son to reign upon his throne; and with the Levites the priests, my ministers. As the host of heaven cannot be numbered, neither the sand of the sea measured: so will I multiply the seed of David my servant, and the Levites that minister unto me.   Jeremiah 33:19-22

God continued to speak to Jeremiah about this matter of covenant and showed him a sign that confirmed His covenant promises and showed their infallibility. This sign showed that we are secure in God because the promises of His Word are sure and unchangeable. Just as long as there is day and night, we can rest in the assurance that God will not fail us. This, then, is a sign of our covenant relationship with a loving heavenly Father.

WHAT IS THE SIGN TO LOOK FOR?

Every time you see darkness coming over the earth, don't be alarmed. It is a sign of your covenant agreement with God and a cause for rejoicing. Rather than be afraid, lift your hands and thank Him.

In the same way, every time you see the sun rising over the horizon, rejoice that God hasn't changed, and your life is secure in His capable hands. He is giving you another day to experience His loving care.

Too often we take the coming of another night or the coming of another day for granted, and we go on our way doing our own thing. But God said that the coming of day and night is a sign of His continued love and care for us, and we should take the opportunity to rejoice in His goodness and remember all that is ours through the covenant.

WHAT DO YOU USUALLY THINK OF?

What do you usually think of when you see night approaching? "I need to hurry and get home before dark," many think or say.

What do you think of when you see another day is dawning? Most people think of all the things they have to do that day, the bills that must be paid, the problems that must be solved. But let's take God at His Word and give thanks for the continuation of His covenant blessings upon our lives, as marked by every new sunrise.

Instead of worrying about the coming day, ask God what He wants you to do with the new covenant day He is granting you. Ask Him who you can bless this covenant day. Then let this covenant reality become part of your daily thinking and, therefore, your daily living.

With the rising of the sun and the going down of the sun, we are reminded of who we are: children of the living God, men and women of covenant, the blessed of the Lord.

GOD IS ALWAYS THERE

The revelation to Jeremiah continued:

Moreover the word of the LORD came to Jeremiah, saying, Considerest thou not what this people have spoken, saying, The two families which the LORD hath chosen, he hath even cast them off? thus they have despised my people, that they should be no more a nation before them. Thus saith the LORD; If my covenant be not with day and night, and if I have not appointed the ordinances of heaven and earth; then will I cast away the seed of Jacob and David my servant, so that I will not take any of his seed to be rulers over the seed of Abraham, Isaac, and Jacob: for I will cause their captivity to return, and have mercy on them.

Jeremiah 33:23-26

God promised not to forget His covenant, and He is still alive today and doing the same with us as He did with the children of Israel in ancient times. Sometimes, when bad things happen to us, we wonder if God is really there. But we should never wonder about that. He is right there by your side, and He is working for your good. If we can only draw near to Him and submit to His will, He will reveal Himself and His presence to us. He said:

Draw nigh to God, and he will draw nigh to you.
James 4:8

Too often, rather than draw near to God we do things and say things that distance us from Him, and then we wonder why we can't feel His presence when we need Him. The key is to develop a covenant relationship with God that secures us in a daily mutually loving relationship and secures our future—whatever may come our way in the days and years to come.

This is the reason I take advantage of every opportunity I get to be in God's presence. If I make an effort to draw nigh to Him, He will never fail to draw nigh to me. If I make an effort to please Him with my daily life, committing to Him my ways and my words, He is there.

Our covenant with God is secure. Rest in this confidence today and begin *Discovering the Untapped Power of Covenant?*

Chapter 4

THE PROMISE OF COVENANT

Now the LORD had said unto Abram, Get thee out of thy country, and from thy kindred, and from thy father's house, unto a land that I will shew thee: and I will make of thee a great nation, and I will bless thee, and make thy name great; and thou shalt be a blessing: and I will bless them that bless thee, and curse him that curseth thee: and in thee shall all families of the earth be blessed. Genesis 12:1-3

What did God say to Abraham?

- *I will make of thee a great nation.*
- *I will bless thee.*
- *I will make thy name great.*
- *I will bless them that bless thee, and curse him that curseth thee.*
- *In thee shall all families of the earth be blessed.*

43

WHAT'S NOT TO LIKE?

What's not to like about those kinds of promises? And what does the world have that could possibly compare to this? God's ways are always best, and we have a legally binding agreement with Him that includes these very promises.

Think about that! God said to Abraham (and He is saying to to you today): "*I will make your name great.*" I didn't say that; God said it. If I said it, I might not be able to fulfill such a promise, but God can do whatever He determines.

If God speaks a thing, He will do it. He keeps His word. He is a covenant-keeping God.

WHAT IS GOD'S DETERMINATION FOR YOUR LIFE?

God has a great plan for your life? Does He perhaps want to make you the mayor of a great city, the governor of a great state, the president or prime minister of a great nation? If so, He can do it very easily.

When you're in covenant with God, you're just one step away from your miracle, whatever it is that God has determined for your life. Therefore it behooves you to keep the covenant and be faithful to God. He will never fail you.

God can do anything but fail. Failure is not within His possibility. If the agreement fails, it will not be His fault. His promises are sure, as He is sure.

THE PROMISE OF COVENANT

WHO IS BEHIND THIS "I"?

Because of who God is, each time He spoke a promise to Abram, it bore His unmistakable mark:

I will make of thee a great nation.
I will bless thee.
I will make thy name great.
I will bless them that bless thee, and curse him that curseth thee.

When God said, *"In thee shall all families of the earth be blessed,"* it was understood that it would happen because of who was saying it, not because Abraham was someone great or someone who deserved such blessings.

Who could promise all of this, and who could fulfill all of this? Not any man, living or dead, but only God Himself.

This is the key to covenant with God. It is based on His character, so it cannot fail, for He cannot fail. It is not dependant upon any man, only on the unfailing God.

YOU WILL TOUCH SO MANY OTHERS

Eventually, the promises to Abraham (and now to you) reached this final level:

In [thee] shall all the families of the earth be blessed.
Genesis 28:14

45

In other words, you will touch so many people in your lifetime and they will touch so many others that no one will remain untouched by your blessed life. Because God said it to Abraham, it was sure in his case, and because the same covenant-keeping God says it to you, it is sure in your case as well.

THEY WILL FEEL JEALOUS

When God has made of you a great nation and made your name great, many may feel jealous and wonder why they were not selected instead. The reason will be that you purposed in your heart to covenant with God, and, knowing He would do His part, you let nothing keep you from doing your part too. That's how covenant works.

Abram accepted God's proposal, and suddenly he had a legal document signed and sealed by the Lord of all lords and King of all kings, and that document promised him blessing everywhere he went and everything he did. No one could prevent it or hinder it in any way, no matter how great they happened to be. A Greater One had cut the covenant with Abram, and that covenant was unchangeable.

NOW IT'S YOUR TURN

The same can be said of the covenant God now offers you. It is a covenant full of promise, and no one can hinder its fulfillment. Will you hear God's voice today and begin to *Discovering the Untapped Power of Covenant?*

Chapter 5

THE RESPONSIBILITY OF COVENANT

Now the LORD had said unto Abram, Get thee out of thy country, and from thy kindred, and from thy father's house, unto a land that I will shew thee: and I will make of thee a great nation, and I will bless thee, and make thy name great; and thou shalt be a blessing: and I will bless them that bless thee, and curse him that curseth thee: and in thee shall all families of the earth be blessed. Genesis 12:1-3

The first thing God spoke to Abram was not a promise on His part, but a responsibility on Abraham's part. The very first thing He said to him was this: "GET OUT."

Get out of where? Abraham had to get out of his country and get away from his family. God wanted to do something new and different for him, and he could not receive it if he remained in the pagan atmosphere of Ur.

ABRAHAM WAS FROM THE GHETTOS

This can be explained by the fact that Abram didn't have a very good upbringing. If he were alive today, he might well have grown up in the ghettos of our modern cities. He might have been from the projects, and his father may have been doing what men did in such places.

Today, the projects are filled with drug dealing, prostitution and crime, and it was no different in Abram's day. He was born into a family that not only worshipped idols; they made idols and sold them to other people to worship.

BORN INTO IDOLATRY

Idolatry has always been a curse. God forbade it from the beginning, and He still forbids it today. The tendency of man is to worship something tangible and visible, but imagine how that hurts the heart of a loving Father who created us all and holds all of creation together by the power of His Word alone.

God calls men out of idolatry, and that's what He did with Abram. He needed a new representative, someone who would stand for him and put forth an example in the Earth, and Abram was his man. This is the reason God told him to get out of the pagan atmosphere of his hometown. There was a better place, a better life, a better tomorrow waiting for him somewhere else, and God promised to show it to him—if he would be willing to do his part.

COVENANT ALWAYS COMES WITH RESPONSIBILITY

Covenant always comes with responsibility. God commits Himself to certain responsibilities that He will faithfully fulfill, but He also requires certain things of us.

The benefits of being in covenant with God are so wonderful that we must do everything we can to be sure that we are walking worthy of our covenant with Him. You must determine today to live and walk in your covenant with God and not let anything cause you to stray from it. His covenants are sure and everlasting. He will not break His covenant with you, and you must not break your agreement with Him.

"GET OUT"

God had a plan for Abram, and He promised him in no uncertain terms, *"I will make of thee a great nation."* But the strength of this promise also placed a requirement upon Abram. *"Get out!"* By this, God meant: change your ways. Get out of the atmosphere of ungodliness and create a new atmosphere in which you, your children and grandchildren can grow and prosper spiritually and physically.

That should be clear enough. If God is going to take you somewhere, there are things you have to leave behind, things you can no longer be a part of. So God is also saying to you today, "Get out!"

Often, when God calls us to a higher level of living, it requires that we leave the company we are presently keeping, our old drinking buddies, the doubters and scoffers who only pull us down and hold us back. They're not going anywhere in life, and if we insist on hanging out with them, we won't go anywhere either.

Every day you are getting a little older, and there is no time to lose. Don't wait until it is too late to make a move for God. It's time to make some serious decisions and enter into some binding agreements with your Creator. It's time for your covenant with the Almighty.

WHAT IT ALL MEANS

If you're willing to get out from your country, your family and your old friends, God has something wonderful He wants to do with you and for you, but this doesn't mean that you have to physically separate from everyone. At one point, I had to have a confrontation with my eldest son. He was coming home late, and I told him if he wanted to live like that, he would have to do it elsewhere.

A few days later, I came home to find a truck parked outside the house, and my son was carrying out a bed I had recently purchased for him and his brother. "Hey, what are you doing?" I asked.

"Well, you told me to leave. So I'm gone!" he answered.

"Okay," I said, "I'll help you take your things out." I gave him some money to help him get started on his own, and before long he was indeed gone.

But life out there was not what my elder son had expected, and for the first time, he now tasted the hardships others know. Just three months later a truck pulled up at the house, and he was moving back home.

Moving out is a serious decision, and it is not to be taken lightly. Abram was being called to make the very serious decisions of getting out of his country, away from kindred, and, most of all, away from the influence of his father's house. "Oh, my God," he must have thought. "What is this You are calling me to do?"

CALLED TO SOME UNNAMED PLACE

To make matters worse, God was calling Abram to some unknown or unnamed place: *"a land that I will shew thee."* But this request was not coming from just anyone. The One offering this covenant was none other than Jehovah, the God of the Universe Himself, and He was saying that if Abram would do his part, he would bring forth more than a great family or family of families. He would birth a great and mighty nation in God.

As we are growing up, one of our greatest dreams is to someday marry and raise a family. Having someone to love us fervently, a beloved spouse, is one of the greatest aspirations of men and women everywhere.

Then, it follows that we want children. This desire, for children to complement a marriage, is fairly universal. Some go so far as to plan exactly how many children they want to have. With some, it's just one or two, but with others, it's five or even ten or more. The thought of spending our last days in the presence of people who love and appreciate us is wonderful. Some of us have our whole lives planned out already, even to how we expect to die.

GOD UPSETS OUR PLANS

We don't like it when God comes and begins to upset our well-thought-out and long-held plans. To us, He seems like an opposing player who suddenly and unexpectedly intercepts the ball and spoils what we thought was a sure goal on our part. The result is that we have to start all over again.

Well, is God really like that? Oh, yes. He wants to interrupt your pilgrimage and put you on a different schedule and a whole new course in life. But … it's for your own good. God always knows what is best for you.

If you let God turn your plans upside down, what does He promise? *"I will bless them that bless thee and curse him that curseth thee: and in thee shall all families of the earth be blessed."* And yet when God changes the course of our lives, we don't like it and neither do those around us. For our part, it seems disruptive, and we feel robbed of our expected future. In reality, that's a foolish way to think. God's plans are always higher than our own, and we never lose anything when we obey His plan for our future.

PUTTING ON AIRS?

Others think that we are suddenly putting on airs, pretending to be something we're not, entertaining foolish dreams of some pie-in-the-sky future. "What kind of games are they playing?" they want to know. But we're not playing games. This is deadly serious business. We want the blessing of God, He has shown us what we must do to get it, and we know that it's worth risking everything else to have it. God NEVER fails. Never! So we have absolutely nothing to lose.

GO FORWARD

If you have entered into a blessed covenant with God, then you've made up your mind to go in the direction He reveals, and nothing and no one is going to stop you. Not many will understand that, but never mind them. Go forward in God and don't look back.

We seem to get discouraged and give up so easily these days. Something unexpected happens or someone offends us, and we fall back and take months (and sometimes years) to recuperate and continue our spiritual journey. This just shows our lack of seriousness with God. If you are committed to Him and you understand His commitment to you, nothing and no one can turn you aside or hold you back. You will push forward through every trial and test. You know that God will not fail you, and you know that you must not fail Him. So keep moving forward and don't let anything or anybody stand in your way.

DOES GOD REALLY WANT
TO GET INVOLVED?

Does God really want to get involved in your business? Oh, yes, He does. He wants to get involved in your family and in everything else that you do. His desire is not to deny you anything or to limit you in any way. He wants you to have the very best, and that's precisely why He gets involved. No one else but Him can give you the best.

Does God want to know what you're doing at any given moment of time? Absolutely! Our parents did that too, and they saved us from much heartache. But God is a better father than any earthly father could ever be. The only reason He wants to know what you're doing all the time is so that He can bless and prosper you in all that you do. It's up to us to be sure we're doing what He can bless and what He can prosper.

"Where are you?" our parents always want to know. "What are you doing?" "Who are you hanging out with?" They're not just being nosey, and they're not trying to limit your fun. They love you and want the very best for you. Could God do any less?

In my own youth, I got to the place, like many, that I no longer volunteered any information to my parents. I told them what I wanted them to know and nothing more. If they asked a specific question, I gave them as little information as possible. I wasn't trying to be rude or cute; I just wanted to do my own thing and didn't want everyone else in my business.

THE DESIRE TO DO YOUR OWN THING

We each seem to come to this attitude at some point in life, usually in our teenage years. Suddenly doing our own thing seems very important. But that's not how covenant with God works. He has great plans for our future, but we have to cooperate with Him and let Him have His way with us. This is an agreement between two parties. God does His part, but you must do yours too.

NEVER ONE SIDED

A covenant is never one-sided. God has committed Himself to me in covenant, and He will never fail to fulfill His part. But I have also made certain promises to Him, and I must keep those promises, just as I expect Him to keep His promises to me. He has promised to keep me and bless me, and my part is to serve Him faithfully day by day, giving Him the glory in all things and always placing His will above my own and all others, come what may. Is it worth all that? Oh, yes, absolutely!

What about you? Why not yield to His will today and begin *Discovering the Untapped Power of Covenant?*

Chapter 6

THE PROCESS OF COVENANT

*But this shall be the covenant that I will make with the house of Israel; After those days, saith the L*ORD*, I will put my law in their inward parts, and write it in their hearts; and will be their God, and they shall be my people.*   Jeremiah 31:33

The whole concept of covenant and the specific covenant we have with our God is powerful. Through covenant, God has established His way of dealing with His people, and He never fails to do His part. This does not mean that things will happen as we expect them to and when we expect them to. There is, with covenant as with most things in life, a process, and each and every one of us is somewhere in that process.

GOD LEADS US STEP-BY-STEP

Step-by-step, God is doing something with us and in us, and each step can and should be, for us, one more victory. But we don't much like any process because a process takes time. We love to do things quickly, instantaneously if possible, but few things of value are created quickly, and none are created instantaneously.

OUR WEAKNESS FOR FAST FOOD

Oh, how we love fast food these days because we have less time to cook. "Just give me a #1 Combo," we say into the microphone at a fast-food restaurant, and it's done. Or we can get a #13 or anything in between.

That is, if you're satisfied with fast food. It's not the best thing for your long-term health, but with our pace of life, that's what more and more people are eating these days.

SEEKING FASTER WAYS TO DO EVERYTHING

It's much the same with other things. We always want to find a quicker way to do it. A good example is the way we wash clothes.

When I was a child, we beat our clothes on a stone to get them clean. Then, we moved up to the washboard, but that also took a lot of time, so when someone invented a washing machine, we adopted it.

The washing machine has gone through many improvements through the years, and nowadays we simply pop our clothes into a machine, leave them for a while, and when we come back, the washer has done all the work, and the clothes are clean. It's not instantaneous, but it is very fast compared to how we had to do it before.

WE LIKE EVERYTHING FAST, BUT GOD'S NOT LIKE THAT

We like everything fast, but God doesn't work like that. He has a process designed for us to pass through, and that process is part of our covenant agreement with Him. He does His part, and He does it in His own way and in His own time, and then we have to do our part.

He promised: *"I will put my law in their inward parts, and write it in their hearts,"* but He does it *"precept upon precept"*:

> *For precept must be upon precept, precept upon precept; line upon line, line upon line; here a little, and there a little.* Isaiah 28:10

This requires that we spend time in God's Word, allowing Him to hide His promises in our hearts. There are no short cuts to victory, and since God is our Creator and Master, He always knows best and determines the way we will go. It is up to us to trust Him and work with Him to see the desired results.

These are the basic foundations of our powerful covenant: God makes great and sure promises, but He places upon us certain requirements, and we must then submit to His prescribed process. So what are we waiting for? Let us submit quickly so that we can begin *Discovering the Untapped Power of Covenant?*

Part II

GOD'S DEALINGS WITH HIS OLD TESTAMENT PEOPLE

Chapter 7

GOD'S COVENANT WITH NOAH

But with thee will I establish my covenant; and thou shalt come into the ark, thou, and thy sons, and thy wife, and thy sons' wives with thee. Genesis 6:18

As we have seen, our God is a covenant maker and a covenant keeper. In ancient times, He made (and kept) a covenant with a man named Noah.

THE ARK AND WHAT IT REPRESENTED

Because of the terrible sin of the people of Noah's time, God was about to destroy the known world, and only those who got into an ark, a type of boat, would be saved from the coming flood. This ark was to be a token of God's covenant, and all who entered into it would be safe.

When Noah came to understand all this, he began to build the required ark and, at the same time, he began to preach, warning his generation of the destruction to come. Like people of every generation (ours included or, perhaps, ours especially), although the people of Noah's day were duly warned, they failed to heed the warning. Noah was preaching something different from what they were accustomed to hearing, so they refused to receive it as truth and obey it.

HEARING A NEW THING

Preaching is different to different hearers. One hears it one way, and another hears it another way. God knows how to speak to the hearts of all men and women.

Often preaching contains warnings, and we need to heed God's warnings. Also we need to be open to new things. To insist that preaching is wrong because it's not what we're accustomed to hearing rules out hearing anything new, and this is sad because God wants to teach us new things.

In Noah's day, God was about to send a flood upon the Earth, and He was using Noah to warn the people so that they could escape the wrath to come. For one hundred and twenty years, Noah preached his heart out, warning anyone who would listen, but even as he preached, the men and women around him mocked and scorned both him and his message.

What was wrong with this CRAZY PREACHER anyway? God would NEVER flood the Earth and drown every living soul! The skeptics were out in number. In fact, they were the majority. Few believed Noah.

GOD HAD A PLAN

But God had a plan. He was making a covenant with Noah, and, as we have seen, His covenants can never be broken. Men may break the covenants they make (and they do), but God cannot. He never has, and He never will! In this covenant, Noah and all his family were to be saved, and they would then begin a new generation upon the Earth. It was assured.

THE COMING OF THE ANIMALS

Eventually, in the process of time, the flood came, but before it did, God spoke to the creatures of the animal kingdom, and pairs of them began to come and get into the ark with Noah. To think that no one noticed animals approaching and entering this strange craft Noah had been building for so long would be naïve. Of course, everyone noticed. This was a rare phenomenon. Still, others did not believe or get onboard the ark.

BUILT AWAY FROM WATER

The ark was a boat, but it was not built on a waterway, where boats of any size are normally constructed. I have noticed, across this country and around the world, that when we get near to any port, there are shipbuilding activities there, but never away from a water source (toward the mountains, for instance). But this boat was different. It was built inland, with no access to a major waterway, and now birds were flying into it, and animals were getting aboard. What could it all mean?

If this happened today, we might think it was some sort of movie, not reality. In that day, I'm not sure what the people thought, but it should have caused them to realize that this was a work of God Himself. This is the way God operates. He speaks, and then He brings what He speaks to pass, regardless of who believes and who doesn't.

NOAH HAD TO DO SOMETHING

Notice that Noah had to do something. He had to build the ark that would serve to rescue himself and his family, and he had to preach and warn others of the impending flood. He was faithful to obey God, so that, even though he was far from perfect, we recognize him today as one of the great heroes of faith.

What about you? Will you accept the offer of blessing the God of covenant is making to you today. Then you can begin *Discovering the Untapped Power of Covenant?*

Chapter 8

GOD'S COVENANT WITH ABRAHAM

Now the LORD had said unto Abram, Get thee out of thy country, and from thy kindred, and from thy father's house, unto a land that I will shew thee: and I will make of thee a great nation, and I will bless thee, and make thy name great; and thou shalt be a blessing: and I will bless them that bless thee, and curse him that curseth thee: and in thee shall all families of the earth be blessed. So Abram departed, as the LORD had spoken unto him; and Lot went with him: and Abram was seventy and five years old when he departed out of Haran. Genesis 12:1-4

As we have seen, God also made a covenant with Abraham, and elements of the Abrahamic covenant are still in effect for us today in our generation. Because Abraham is the inspiration for this message, we will give his story more space, and so we have read again the promise God made him.

TWENTY YEARS LATER

Then, some twenty years later, God spoke to Abram again and offered him a second covenant promise:

> *In the same day the L*ORD *made a covenant with Abram, saying, Unto thy seed have I given this land, from the river of Egypt unto the great river, the river Euphrates: the Kenites, and the Kenizzites, and the Kadmonites, And the Hittites, and the Perizzites, and the Rephaims, And the Amorites, and the Canaanites, and the Girgashites, and the Jebusites.*
>
> Genesis 15:18-21

TWENTY-FOUR YEARS AFTER THAT

Twenty-four years after that, when Abraham was already ninety-nine years old, another covenant promise came to him:

> *And when Abram was ninety years old and nine, the L*ORD *appeared to Abram, and said unto him, I am the Almighty God; walk before me, and be thou perfect. And I will make my covenant between me and thee, and will multiply thee exceedingly.*
> *And Abram fell on his face: and God talked with him, saying, As for me, behold, my covenant is with thee,*

and thou shalt be a father of many nations. Neither shall thy name any more be called Abram, but thy name shall be Abraham; for a father of many nations have I made thee. And I will make thee exceeding fruitful, and I will make nations of thee, and kings shall come out of thee. And I will establish my covenant between me and thee and thy seed after thee in their generations for an everlasting covenant, to be a God unto thee, and to thy seed after thee. And I will give unto thee, and to thy seed after thee, the land wherein thou art a stranger, all the land of Canaan, for an everlasting possession; and I will be their God.

And God said unto Abraham, Thou shalt keep my covenant therefore, thou, and thy seed after thee in their generations. This is my covenant, which ye shall keep, between me and you and thy seed after thee; Every man child among you shall be circumcised. Genesis 17:1-10

"WALK BEFORE ME AND BE THOU PERFECT"

"Walk before me, and be thou perfect." What a strange thing to tell a man who was already ninety-nine years old. Wasn't it a little late for that? What was God trying to say to Abraham? He was trying to let him know that the covenant, or agreement, that He had made with him so many years before (when he was a much younger man), was still just as valid as it had ever been. The promises of God were not diminishing with age. In fact, they were growing even more incredible. God said:

69

And I will make my covenant between me and thee, and will multiply thee exceedingly. Genesis 17:2

Personally, I've never known a man as old as Abraham who was able to have children, but God is great. He does the impossible.

WHAT TOOK SO LONG?

What took so long for God's covenant with Abraham to be fulfilled? It seems that after Abraham first heard from God on this matter, he must have begun to examine his situation and to wonder if he had really heard from God. He was, after all, already an old man, and his wife had been barren from the start of their marriage. So that presented some rather impossible situations.

From time to time, God tells us things that seem incredible—to us and others—and we have to wonder if we're maybe having a mid-life crisis or something and not really hearing form Heaven.

Sometimes God will tell you to do some things that are not normal, and you may be tempted to doubt if it really is God speaking. To show Abraham that he was hearing from the Almighty Himself and that He was serious, God spoke of the holy covenant between them.

WHAT DID GOD WANT TO DO?

What did God want to do for and through this man Abraham? Satan had spoiled the perfection of the Garden of Eden and the innocence of the man and woman who dwelled there and their relationship to their Creator, and this adversely affected every succeeding generation. Now God wanted to reestablish His presence on the Earth, which He had created and among the creatures He had created. Something glorious was about to happen, if Abraham was willing to covenant with God.

WHAT WERE THE TERMS OF THE AGREEMENT?

What were the terms of this agreement? First, God would give Abraham a son through his own wife, Sarai. We must remember that he already had one son, Ishmael, born of the Egyptian handmaiden named Hagar, but Ishmael was not the son of promise. Now Sarai, at ninety years of age, was given a new name. From that time on she would be known as Sarah, mother of nations, and very quickly things began to happen.

So if God tells you something that seems incredible, don't kill it with your unbelief. Trust God. He delights in doing the impossible, and He wants to do it for you today, just as He did for Abraham so long ago.

FORSAKING YOUR WAYS

God now promised:

In the same day the LORD made a covenant with Abram, saying, Unto thy seed have I given this land,

71

from the river of Egypt unto the great river, the river
Euphrates: the Kenites, and the Kenizzites, and the
Kadmonites, and the Hittites, and the Perizzites, and
the Rephaims, and the Amorites, and the Canaanites,
and the Girgashites, and the Jebusites.

Genesis 15:18-22

God was saying to Abraham, "If you will be willing to leave your country and the security of your father's house, I will make a covenant with you, to sustain you, acting as your Father." What does this mean to us today? Through this, God is saying to us, "If you can just get out of yourself and out of your own ways, I will do marvels for you." Wow!

Each of us has his or her own ways, and those ways are not God's ways. Each of us has his or her own thoughts, and those thoughts are not God's thoughts. If we can just get out of ourselves, away from our own ways and our own limited thoughts, God can do something wonderful for us and through us. God is ready to give us things we've never had before, but He's waiting for us to get out of ourselves so that He can work.

Some new territory was waiting for Abraham and his descendants, if he could only see his way clear to step out on faith and trust God as never before. That is also our challenge today.

TIME PASSED, BUT THE CALL DID NOT CHANGE

When God first made this proposition to Abraham, he was already about seventy-five years old. Then more time passed, and when God next spoke in this way to him, he was nearing the century mark:

> *And when Abram was ninety years old and nine, the* LORD *appeared to Abram, and said unto him, I am the Almighty God; walk before me, and be thou perfect. And I will make my covenant between me and thee, and will multiply thee exceedingly.*
>
> *And Abram fell on his face: and God talked with him, saying, As for me, behold, my covenant is with thee, and thou shalt be a father of many nations. Neither shall thy name any more be called Abram, but thy name shall be Abraham; for a father of many nations have I made thee. And I will make thee exceeding fruitful, and I will make nations of thee, and kings shall come out of thee. And I will establish my covenant between me and thee and thy seed after thee in their generations for an everlasting covenant, to be a God unto thee, and to thy seed after thee. And I will give unto thee, and to thy seed after thee, the land wherein thou art a stranger, all the land of Canaan, for an everlasting possession; and I will be their God.*
>
> Genesis 17:1-8

In the first call, God told Abraham (still Abram) he had to get out of his father's house, out of his country, out of his earthly habits, out of his self life. Now the call deepened, and God called Abram to walk before Him and be perfect.

GOD WANTS TO SEE SOME CHANGE IN YOUR WALK

When God calls you out of yourself, He wants to see some change in your walk. He wants to see that you are moving toward the goal of perfection. He wants to see that you are maturing spiritually.

Just as with children, some people seem to grow up very quickly in the things of God, while others seem to take a long time to mature. If Abram was willing to step out of himself and move toward maturity in God, God had many wonderful things in store for him. He would not only make His covenant with Abram; He would *"multiply [him] exceedingly."*

Abram liked the sound of that, and so he fell on his face before God. This released God to continue to reveal His promises. His covenant would be with Abram, and Abram would become the father of many nations.

WHAT COULD IT ALL MEAN?

What could all of this mean? Could Abram have fully understood it all? Probably not! What we can say is that he fully understood that something great was about to happen in his life, and I can make that same statement to you today. If you are willing to enter into covenant with the God of Abraham, great things are about to happen in your life as well. If you can just keep your hand on the plow, remain focused, and keep walking with God, great things lie just ahead. Believe it, and you will see it come to pass, for the God of covenant is faithful.

GOD'S COVENANT WITH ABRAHAM

There are many distractions, on the right and on the left, and many things that would try to move you aside out of the way of blessing. But if you will insist on continuing to walk before the Lord, moving steadily toward maturity and perfection, nothing will be able to hinder you.

A NAME CHANGE

The change God was calling for in Abram's life was so severe that He also called for his name to be changed. He was no longer to be known as Abram, but he would, from then on, be called Abraham (meaning father of many). God wants to change you so totally that you will be unrecognizable. He wants to change your entire outlook on life and your way of expressing yourself. Your change will be so complete that you will also need a new name, for you'll no longer be the same person.

Abram was the man who had come out of a place called Ur of the Chaldees, but Abram was no more. A new man had emerged, the man known as Abraham, a man of faith and promise. Abram had been limited by his circumstances and his surroundings, but this new man would be a father of many, and God would make him *"exceedingly fruitful."*

HOW COULD HE BE SO FRUITFUL?

How could a man of nearly one hundred years of age be fruitful? That's the wonderful thing about God. He can do what no one else can do. We, however, have hindered Him by our doubts and fears. You are the one who says "I cannot." God never said that about you.

God says you can, and no matter what doctors say, you can because God said it. He always has the last word. It doesn't matter what things look like, God always has the last word. It doesn't matter how depleted your bank account may be, you can be what God says you can be, and you can do what God says you can do.

As Jesus said:

A man's life consisteth not in the abundance of the things which he possesseth.   Luke 12:15

YOUR WORLDLY SUCCESS MEANS NOTHING TO GOD

On the other hand, you may have a lot, and you may have achieved a lot in life, but that means nothing to God. He knows how to take someone with nothing and begin to elevate them. His promise is this:

When a man's ways please the LORD, he maketh even his enemies to be at peace with him.
Proverbs 16:7

When your way begins to please God, He will begin to open to you doors and avenues that you have never yet dreamed of. Stop limiting Him.

WE HAVE LIMITED GOD

God is not limited, and yet you and I have limited Him. The Psalmist declared:

Yea, they turned back and tempted God, and limited the Holy One of Israel.　　Psalm 78:41

How have we limited the Holy One of Israel? By failing to take the Word of God and apply it to our daily lives. Many parts of His Word seem much too old-fashioned for our modern minds. We no longer believe many of the things that previous generations held as solid and irrevocable truths.

Our thinking has changed, even in the past ten years. "This is a scientific age," people insist. "We can no longer go on faith. We must depend on our technology, not on God." But no matter how advanced the technology of the age becomes, God is always greater. We haven't discovered anything that He didn't create in the first place. We're just finally understanding what He knew long ago. That's all. Technology does not make Him out of date. He is technology, and there would be no technology without Him.

NATIONS AND KINGS WOULD COME FROM HIM

Abram (now Abraham) would not only be exceedingly fruitful. Nations would come out of him, and so would kings. This speaks of a legacy, and because these promises came to Abraham through covenant, no one would be able to stop them or hinder them in any way.

In New Testament times we who are of the household of faith are called the children of Abraham, and this is no less true of our current generations, with all of our high-tech gadgetry. Therefore, we can also lay hold of the same promises, if we can just push aside our doubts.

FULL OF DOUBTS

Like us, Abraham began to put forth all the reasons that what God was saying could not happen. He was already old. How could a *"seed"* come forth from a ninety-nine-year-old man? Sarah was ninety, an age Abraham described as *"stricken with age."* How could she bear a child now? Should they adopt perhaps? But God assured Abraham that the child He had promised would come forth in the normal way, even though Abraham and Sarah were both well beyond the normal childbearing age.

And, wonder of wonders, it happened just as God had said! At ninety, Sarah became pregnant. That had to be particularly awesome for a woman of her age and for a man of nearly one hundred years of age. Abraham was still virulent, but only because God was intervening in his situation.

THE WHY OF ISAAC

Do you know why this particular child had to be born, why God allowed this man and this woman to know the joys of bearing a child in their old age? It was because their seed would carry the sacred line all the way down to Jesus, the Messiah and Savior of the world. Through the lineage of Isaac, the son of Abraham and Sarah, and then through Isaac's son Jacob and Jacob's son Joseph, both Joseph (of Nazareth) and Mary, who were to bring Jesus into this world, would be born. Through the unusual birth of Isaac God was setting up the affairs of this world, making way for the coming of the Savior of all mankind.

That was the reason Abraham was warned not to try to deviate from what God was telling him. Sarah was going to have a baby, and that was the end of the discussion. Their age meant nothing at all to God. It was all part of the covenant that could not fail.

CAN YOU SEE?

Can you see how important a covenant is? I hope so because God has something very special in mind for you too. Join yourself to Him in covenant today, do your part, and you will see the glorious end result, just as Abraham did. Begin today *Discovering the Untapped Power of Covenant.*

Chapter 9

GOD'S COVENANT WITH SARAH

And God said unto Abraham, As for Sarai thy wife,
thou shalt not call her name Sarai, but Sarah shall her
name be. And I will bless her, and give thee a son also
of her: yea, I will bless her, and she shall be a mother
of nations; kings of people shall be of her.

Genesis 17:15-16

Sarai, Abraham's wife, had her part in this coming blessing. She, too, was part of the covenant.

The problem was that God said she and Abraham would have a son, but she was barren (and old). Because of this, people mocked her everywhere she went.

BARRENNESS WAS A CURSE

In those days, barrenness was considered to be a curse, and women who suffered it were ostracized from society.

Sarai no doubt suffered the constant sneers of those she met in the affairs of daily life. Many hurtful things were surely said about her, but now God was giving her a very different kind of word. Something was about to change. God was saying that He would bless her, where once she had been cursed with barrenness.

This called for a name change in her too. As Sarah, the previously barren woman would not only bear a son; she would become *"a mother of nations,"* and kings would come forth from her. No longer cursed, her blessing would be evident to everyone who knew her, and now a very different kind of thing would be said of her.

A WORD THAT CANNOT FAIL

All that God was saying in that moment seemed so incredible to Sarah (and it would have to you too), but when something is part of God's covenant, no man and no devil can touch it. It is assured. God seals His covenant promises, and no one can prevent them from coming to pass. So when God speaks a thing, it is as good as done. It's only a matter of time.

Many of the ancient kings, including the pharaoh's of Egypt and the leaders of the Babylonian and Persian empires, were so powerful that when they spoke something or commanded something to be written it was then considered unchangeable (even by them). But the power of these ancient kings and rulers could never be compared to the power of our God. When He speaks a thing, it is done. Finished! Completed!

Sarah experienced this truth, despite the very difficult circumstances of her life, and you can experience it too. Your circumstances are not impossible for God. He does the impossible. Why not begin today *Discovering the Untapped Power of Covenant.*

Chapter 10

GOD'S COVENANT WITH DAVID

Now these be the last words of David. David the son of Jesse said, and the man who was raised up on high, the anointed of the God of Jacob, and the sweet psalmist of Israel, said, The Spirit of the LORD spake by me, and his word was in my tongue. The God of Israel said, the Rock of Israel spake to me, He that ruleth over men must be just, ruling in the fear of God. And he shall be as the light of the morning, when the sun riseth, even a morning without clouds; as the tender grass springing out of the earth by clear shining after rain. Although my house be not so with God; yet he hath made with me an everlasting covenant, ordered in all things, and sure: for this is all my salvation, and all my desire, although he make it not to grow.

2 Samuel 23:1-5

A MAN OF EXPERIENCE

God not only made covenants with Noah, Abraham and Sarah; He also made a covenant with David (among many others). These were the words of a man of experience. At one point, David declared:

> *I have been young, and now am old; yet have I not seen the righteous forsaken, nor his seed begging bread.*   Psalm 37:25

Clearly David knew what it was to keep his eyes focused on God, the Creator, even though he sometimes made personal mistakes.

DAVID MADE MISTAKES

David was not always been the man he should have been. He made mistakes, and there were evident flaws in his character (just as there are in ours). But with all of his flaws, David had a heart fixed on God. When speaking to the haughty King Saul, the prophet Samuel said of David (then a young man, but the man who would replace Saul as king):

> *But now thy kingdom shall not continue: the LORD hath sought him a man after his own heart, and the LORD hath commanded him to be captain over his people, because thou hast not kept that which the LORD commanded thee.*   1 Samuel 13:14

God called David a man after His own heart. He knew, from the start, all of David's flaws, and yet He made a covenant with him and set him over Israel, to rule as her king. And he used David to teach us all to worship, through his wonderful Psalms.

GOD CALLED DAVID HIS SON

God was not ashamed to call David His son. No wonder David could say: *"the Rock of Israel spake to me."* Why? Because he was not arrogant, as leaders often tend to become. It is possible to be firm and decisive and still have the love of God flowing from you so that others see it and marvel.

Today we desperately need leaders, like David, who will not bend under the pressure of every situation but will stand firm in the face of any and every enemy. David could be such a man because God had made with him an everlasting covenant. How awesome!

What about you today? Why not begin now *Discovering the Untapped Power of Covenant?*

Part III

WHAT GOD'S COVENANT IS LIKE TODAY

Chapter 11

GOD'S COVENANT WITH YOU

Now the LORD had said unto Abram, Get thee out of thy country, and from thy kindred, and from thy father's house, unto a land that I will shew thee: and I will make of thee a great nation, and I will bless thee, and make thy name great; and thou shalt be a blessing: and I will bless them that bless thee, and curse him that curseth thee: and in thee shall all families of the earth be blessed. Genesis 12:1-3

We have firmly established that God made a covenant with Abraham (formerly Abram), and part of the promise of that covenant was this: *I will make of thee a great nation.*

WHAT A PROMISE!

Wow! What a promise! God didn't just promise Abraham a family or a community of families, but He promised him an entire nation of families. How awesome is our God and His ways!

These families would come forth from Abraham, and yet he would be the principle figure among them. He would be the focal point, the example others would look to, of what God could do with a willing man or woman, and God is calling men and women today to fulfill the same role in society.

The whole point of examining some of these Old Testament covenants is just to see what they are like, for now it's your turn. God wants to establish a covenant with YOU.

NOW IT'S YOUR TURN

You may find it hard to believe, but I want to declare through the pages of this book that God is making to you the very same promise He made to Abraham so long ago. Regardless of what type of family you came from, what type of education you received or what your particular calling in life, God wants to bring forth from you a great harvest in the Earth. He is calling you to be an example that others can look to and know how to model their own behavior.

You might not be extremely well educated, and yet great men and women can come forth from you. Doctors and lawyers, police commissioners and judges can spring forth from your godly example. God can take your life and transform it and answer the age-old question: Can any good thing come out of this place and this situation?

You're the answer to that difficult question. Yes, it can, by the grace and mercy of God. It can. God can do it.

MY OWN HUMBLE BACKGROUND

I, like many of you, came from a background of very low self-esteem. We had some successful people in our family, but they were the exception and not the rule, and there were not enough of them to inspire the rest of us.

As a young person, I didn't have many role models to look to, for there were a whole lot of things going on around me that I could not approve of.

Many of you have come out of an environment of alcoholism or drug abuse, sexual perversion or crime, and you feel fortunate just to be alive, just to have escaped that poisonous atmosphere. What is important is not the past but what we are doing to change all that and give our children and grandchildren a better future than we had at their age. This can be ours because of the covenant God offers us today.

IT'S PERSONAL

All this talk of covenant is important because God's covenant is for YOU. He is saying to you today, "I will bless YOU! I will make YOUR name great! I will make of YOU a great nation." Believe it, and say yes to God today, and then get started on your glorious future. Begin now *Discovering the Untapped Power of Covenant.*

Chapter 12

COVENANT AND FAMILY

And in thy seed shall all the nations of the earth be blessed; because thou hast obeyed my voice.

Genesis 22:18

God makes covenants with certain nations, with certain generations and with certain individuals. His will is that the promised blessings flow down from one generation to the next through families, so keeping covenant with God is very important for the destiny of your family. What you do will affect not just yourself, but many others around you—even for many generations to come.

GOD IS AT WORK AMONG FAMILIES

We can sometimes see families in which there have been no preachers, and suddenly one member of that family will feel called and will be raised up. This shows that God has been working with that family for a long time, even though we might not yet have seen the evidence of it. He ordained long ago that an anointed voice would come forth from that lineage, and it happens as He has determined.

IT HAPPENED TO ME

I know it happens because it happened to me. I never personally knew of any preachers in our family, either on my mother's side or my father's side. There were bakers, tailors, barbers, policemen and even a police commissioner (and many others), but no preachers. So when God raised me up as a minister, it came as a shock to the whole family.

Our family loved to party, so I was in parties every night and loved it. That didn't seem to be a very good preparation for the ministry. But then something suddenly changed in me, and I was a new person. It was so sudden and so unexpected that I couldn't explain it.

MINDING MY OWN BUSINESS

I was minding my own business one day when someone met me on the street and invited me to a church service. "Oh, I'm sorry," I said. "We're Catholic, and we don't attend other churches." But, despite my protests, I went that night, and in that place something happened to me. I was arrested by God. It seemed that He had been looking for me for a very long time, and when I came along, like Adam, He called out to me: "Where art thou?"

Many of you were also hidden, but God found you. He knows your name, your age, your height and description. He knows where you live and what your telephone number is. And He knows everything else about you as well.

God knows more about you than you know about yourself. Do you doubt that? Well, He even knows how many hairs you have on your head. Did you know that? Jesus said:

> *But the very hairs of your head are all numbered.*
> Matthew 10:30

God knows the end from the beginning and everything in between. He knows absolutely everything about your life, and there is nothing you can tell Him that would surprise Him.

NOTHING SURPRISES GOD

We hear things that surprise us frequently, but not God. He already knows it before it becomes common gossip and reaches our ears.

We even get shocked over news that should cause us to rejoice, that wandering children have come home to God. He never forsook them, even when they forsook Him, and we thank God that they are now home where they belonged all along.

It continues to surprise us that certain people are

serving God, but it should not surprise us. They were born to serve Him. The devil wants us to believe that he has control over our lives and that he can do with us as he wills, but God is still on His throne.

KEEP COVENANT WITH GOD

When we are tempted to do what others are doing, we must remember our covenant with God and its affect upon our family. We made a promise that we must keep.

For God's part, He has kept His promises to us. Now the blessing of many generations of people depends upon our decision to keep covenant with Him.

We were not destined to wander in barren places; we were destined to serve the Lord, destined for greatness in Him, and this greatness is to be passed down to the coming generations.

Covenant is a family thing, and, in this way, you can change the course of history for coming generations. Why not begin today *Discovering the Untapped Power of Covenant?*

Chapter 13

THE NEW COVENANT IN CHRIST'S BLOOD

But now hath he obtained a more excellent ministry, by how much also he is the mediator of a better covenant, which was established upon better promises. For if that first covenant had been faultless, then should no place have been sought for the second. For finding fault with them, he saith, Behold, the days come, saith the Lord, when I will make a new covenant with the house of Israel and with the house of Judah: not according to the covenant that I made with their fathers in the day when I took them by the hand to lead them out of the land of Egypt; because they continued not in my covenant, and I regarded them not, saith the Lord. For this is the covenant that I will make with the house of Israel after those days, saith the Lord; I will put my laws into their mind, and write them in their hearts: and I will be to them a God, and they shall be to me a people. Hebrews 8:6-10

Every covenant God ever made was understood to be eternal, unbreakable, unchanging, and irrevocable, and each of them looked forward to the coming of Christ and what we now call the New Covenant in His blood.

DAVID'S COVENANT LOOKED FORWARD TO CHRIST

In David's day, for instance, the covenant he made with God was more than just an agreement for him to reign over his people. It was also about the eventual coming of a Savior into the world, and the blessings that you and I now enjoy in Christ. David often prophesied of that very event. And, as we have seen, this same thing could be said of the other Old Testament covenants.

The covenant with Christ would be the culmination of all covenants, the Granddaddy of them all. Those who sat in darkness were about to see a great light, and those who sat in sin could look up and behold the power and the glory of the living God. It would come through David's seed.

We, therefore, are living in the very best of times. We have no reason to wish to go back to live in Abraham's time, or David's time or even the time when the disciples walked the Earth with Jesus in the flesh. We now have the best of all offers from God. His promises were never greater.

NO GREATER COVENANT

There is no greater covenant, no greater offer, no greater promise. What our God offers us in Christ is the best of the best. We are privileged to live in this, the best of all times, and to partake of these matchless covenant promises.

So what are you waiting for? Why not begin today. Start *Discovering the Untapped Power of Covenant.*

Part IV

THE LINK BETWEEN COVENANT AND LOVE

Chapter 14

THE LOVE THAT FORGED THIS AMAZING COVENANT

For God so loved the world, that he gave his only begotten Son, that whosoever believeth in him should not perish, but have everlasting life. John 3:16

The love of God is one of the most extensive topics in the Bible, mentioned some 185 times in the Scriptures. It is summed up in this, one of our very favorite verses.

As I examine the Scriptures on this subject, I notice that there are various manifestations of love. For instance, there is a love of compassion, a love of warning, a love of goodness, and a love of invitation. All of these types of love have been extended to us, and now we are called to exhibit them toward others.

THE VARIED MANIFESTATIONS OF GOD'S LOVE

A love of compassion is self-explanatory, but what is a love of invitation? When you get out in the highways and byways of life and begin to compel men and women to come into the Kingdom, that is a love of invitation. Because you love people you meet everywhere (and God loves them), you don't want to see them die and go into a Christless eternity. This compels you to make every effort to win them to Christ.

What is a love of goodness? Such a love compels you to do kind deeds for others in need.

Many are in search of love today, genuine love, and exactly what such a love is all about. What they need is clearly the matchless and endless love of God, manifest through you and me, His children and representatives on the Earth.

A TIMELESS EXPRESSION OF LOVE

In 1917, Frederick M. Lehman wrote the words of the wonderful and timeless hymn, *The Love of God*. His hymn had only two verses. According to TimelessTruths. org, what came to be the beloved verse 3 was "penciled on the wall of a narrow room in an insane asylum by a man said to have been demented. The profound lines were discovered when they laid him in his coffin." Imagine a man in such a situation writing these words:

Could we with ink the ocean fill,
And were the skies of parchment made,
Were every stalk on earth a quill,
And every man a scribe by trade;
To write the love of God above
Would drain the ocean dry;
Nor could the scroll contain the whole,
Though stretched from sky to sky.

What beautiful and powerful words! If we were to try to fully express the love of God that made this wonderful covenant possible, we would continually be looking for more ink, and no dictionary in the world has enough words to fully express and explain such a great love.

There is a human love, and we understand that better, but here we're talking about the fathomless love that sent Jesus to die for us on Calvary. Today, far too many, when they seek love, are caught up in the worldly love, when what they really need is what you and I have to share with them, love eternal, love sublime, the matchless love of Jesus.

NO WORLDLY LOVE CAN MATCH IT

When men go in search of erotic love, they wake up the next morning with their mouth smelling like the bottom of a parrot's cage, and yet they're still not satisfied. You and I, on the other hand, know where real love lies, and we can join each other in the House of God and thank Him who *"is love,"* that because of His love for us, we are alive and well and rejoicing as members of His loving family and enjoying all the benefits of His Kingdom.

The chorus of that wonderful hymn rings just as true today as it did when it was first penned, nearly 100 years ago:

Oh, love of God, how rich and pure!
How measureless and strong!
It shall forevermore endure—
The saints' and angels' song.

Paul wrote to the Corinthian believers:

For the love of Christ constraineth us; because we thus judge, that if one died for all, then were all dead:
1 Corinthians 5:14

THE SAME LOVE THAT MOVED JESUS MUST MOVE US

It was love that moved Jesus to minister to those in need while He was here on this earth:

But when he saw the multitudes, he was moved with compassion on them, because they fainted, and were scattered abroad, as sheep having no shepherd.
Matthew 9:36

And Jesus went forth, and saw a great multitude, and was moved with compassion toward them, and he healed their sick.
Matthew 14:14

108

THE LOVE THAT FORGED THIS AMAZING COVENANT

And Jesus, moved with compassion, put forth his hand, and touched him, and saith unto him, I will; be thou clean.　　　　　Mark 1:41

When you and I look out into the world, we must see men and women as Jesus saw them. May God give us eyes of faith to see what men and women can become, not what they have fallen to. We are to walk as Jesus walked in this world, and we are to think as He thought, for we are now His representatives on the Earth. Jesus is not here now, but we are here in His stead. He wants to love men and women through you.

YOUR PRESENCE MAKES A DIFFERENCE

Someone may say, "If Jesus were here, things would be different." Well I'm here, and things are different because of it. You're here, and things are different because of it. We are His ambassadors of love. He extended this love to each of us, and now, in gratitude, we must bring it to others.

When you go on your job, things change because the love of God is in you. I remember arriving at one job, and there was total chaos. Everyone was fussing and cussing at each other, and many harsh things were being said. I passed on through to the back, not being willing to be part of that type of conversation, and bowed my head and said, "God, this not good."

Then, before long, I heard someone say, "The preacher's here," and then, in a moment, "We're going to have

109

to change our conversation." Sure enough, before long I heard the very same people talking about Adam and Eve and then Cain and where he got his wife. I hadn't said a word, but my very presence changed things that day.

Stand strong as a believer and don't get tired and fall back into your old ways, and you will change things around you. Being a Christian is wonderful and exciting, and employers need more Christians working for them. If they have no Christians, they will go broke because of employee theft. Because of God's love in us, we are the salt (or preservative) of the Earth.

YOU ARE SALT AND LIGHT TO THE WORLD

The Bible calls us light and salt, and that's what we must be everywhere we go. I was in New York City once during a great snowstorm, and the only thing that could help clear the roads and give the vehicles traction was salt, so they had the salt trucks out in force. You're salt, too, and wherever you go, things should change.

YOU ARE FAR MORE IMPORTANT THAN YOU CAN POSSIBLY KNOW

You are far more important than you can possibly know. Tell yourself that today.

Although we sometimes feel like we are less than nothing, we are very precious and valuable in God's sight.

We pull ourselves down by our poor self-image, our grass-hopper mentality.

GET RID OF YOUR GRASSHOPPER MENTALITY

When Joshua sent the spies to check out the land of Canaan, they came back with the report, "When we saw the people, how big they are, we seemed like grasshoppers in comparison." That's what your poor self-image will do, make you believe that you are like a grasshopper, when, in reality, you are a giant of love.

When you are walking with the King of kings and Lord of lords, the God of all love, and you still feel like a nobody, something is wrong. We must never allow situations and circumstances to put us so low that we feel like a nobody and walk with our heads hanging down, lamenting, "Poor me, I don't know what to do. It's all over." No! It's not over yet! The Scriptures promise:

> *Ye are of God, little children, and have overcome them: because greater is he that is in you, than he that is in the world.* 1 John 4:4

MAKE IT PERSONAL

I make that personal: "Greater is He that is in ME than he that is in the world." I have something that the world can't give and the world can't take it away. I have the overcoming Christ abiding in me. I have the Holy Ghost

111

who leads and guides me every single day of my life. And I have God's great love working in me. So never accept the lie that you are a nobody; that's what the devil wants you to believe. You are a giant of faith and love.

GET HAPPY

We Christians often go around looking very solemn and sad, when, in reality, we are the King's kids. We sometimes dress like paupers, when our God wants the very best for us.

With our long faces, we have developed a new anthem for the Christian church today. Instead of the classic anthem, *When the Saints Go Marching In*, we are now forced to sing: *When the Saints Go Dragging In.*

But who wants to be in that number? Not me. I want to be somewhere exciting, where something is moving, something is happening. I want to be where God is working and changing things and where His love is at work. Saints, it's time to move on deeper into this matchless love of God and let it fulfill the promise of covenant in us and then enable us to reach out with love to others.

Start today. Begin now *Discovering the Untapped Power of Covenant.*

Chapter 15

JESUS' STUNNING CONCLUSIONS ON LOVE

But I say unto you which hear, Love your enemies, do good to them which hate you, bless them that curse you, and pray for them which despitefully use you. And unto him that smiteth thee on the one cheek offer also the other; and him that taketh away thy cloak forbid not to take thy coat also. Give to every man that asketh of thee; and of him that taketh away thy goods ask them not again.

And as ye would that men should do to you, do ye also to them likewise. For if ye love them which love you, what thank have ye? for sinners also love those that love them. And if ye do good to them which do good to you, what thank have ye? for sinners also do even the same. And if ye lend to them of whom ye hope to receive, what thank have ye? for sinners also lend to sinners, to receive as much again.

But love ye your enemies, and do good, and lend, hoping for nothing again; and your reward shall be great, and ye shall be the children of the Highest: for he is kind unto the unthankful and to the evil. Be ye therefore merciful, as your Father also is merciful. Judge not, and ye shall not be judged: condemn not, and ye shall not be condemned: forgive, and ye shall be forgiven: give, and it shall be given unto you; good measure, pressed down, and shaken together, and running over, shall men give into your bosom. For with the same measure that ye mete withal it shall be measured to you again.   Luke 6:27-38

A very critical part of our New Testament Covenant is love, Kingdom love, God's love, and on this subject, Jesus spoke these amazing, seemingly-impossible-to-fulfill words in His Sermon on the Mount.

TO WHOM IS IT ADDRESSED?

Love your enemies, do good to them which hate you.
                                        Verse 27

These are commands, but they are addressed to *"you which hear."* Not everyone will be willing to hear, much less obey, these kinds of commands. What Jesus was saying may seem impossible to many, if not most, but if Jesus said it, then it's not only possible; it's law for those of us who love Him, share His covenant promises and make up His Kingdom here on the Earth.

114

LOVE YOUR ENEMIES?

Many would not consider it a very nice thing to do to suggest that they have to love their enemies. They would complain, "But they have done me wrong. They hurt me. Everything I'm going through right now is because of what they did to me." This may be something that was done to them recently, but often it is something that was done many months or even many years ago, and yet that person is still suffering because of it. And now you have the nerve to tell them that they have to love their enemies?

That doesn't sound very good to them, considering the circumstances. But the stark truth is that you will never be successful as a Christian if you fail to exhibit the love of God in your life and character, regardless of what other people do or have done to you.

BLESS THEM ... PRAY FOR THEM

What did Jesus say to do when people offend you?

Bless them that curse you.   Verse 28

You may think I'm losing my mind by even suggesting such a thing, but these are not my words. They're Jesus' words. He went even further:

And pray for them which despitefully use you.
                                                  Verse 28

Some people don't just *"use"* us once. They use us over and over again. How, then, can we forgive them for such grievous and continued wrongs?

Most of us would say, "If they use me once, I may be excused for allowing it, but if they go on and use me several times, then I would be stupid if I didn't stand up against them." But Jesus said nothing of how many times a person has used you. He just said *"pray for them."*

Yes, they know they're doing wrong, and they continue to do it. But you just need to go for the ride.

THE JOURNEY IS IMPORTANT

The journey is important, every bit as important as the final destination. Get ready for the ride.

When those of us who live in Baton Rouge want to go north to Shreveport, we have to first pass through Alexandria and other smaller cities of Louisiana, but because we're going somewhere we behave ourselves well in each of those places. And, Beloved, we are definitely going somewhere in God, so don't be lax in the journey.

The place we are headed is so exciting and so wonderful that it would be wrong of us to think that we can just stroll in there. We'll have to leap over some hurdles, climb some mountains, surmount some barriers and fight the devil at every turn to get to where we're going. Our final destination is just that wonderful, and we must not let anything keep us from reaching it!

HELP EACH OTHER ALONG THE WAY

Getting to our destination is so important that we need to help each other along the way, and that is one of the major responsibilities of the Church today, helping God's people to reach their full potential, their final destiny and final destination. Where you are going is important, but you must make the journey in covenant love and help others to make it too.

Some Christians have come to the conclusion that it's okay for them to cuss somebody out and walk away feeling no shame or hurt for having done it. But true Christians don't act like that. Instead, true Christians exhibit the love of God to all those around them. True Christians know how to hold their peace when they have been offended. Instead of cussing someone out, they pray for them. They bless them. That's what Jesus taught as covenant love. God loved us when we were not worthy of love, so He commands us to love others, whether they deserve our love or not.

OFFER ALSO THE OTHER

Jesus went ever further:

And unto him that smiteth thee on the one cheek offer also the other; and him that taketh away thy cloak forbid not to take thy coat also. Give to every man that asketh of thee; and of him that taketh away thy goods

117

ask them not again. And as ye would that men should do to you, do ye also to them likewise.   Verses 29-31

What? This can't be right, can it? If a man hits me on one side of my face, God wants me to offer him the other side so he can hit me there too? That doesn't sound right, and yet that seems to be exactly what Jesus was saying here.

When someone has taken something from me, I am to allow them to take something else? That can't be right, can it? And yet that seems to be what Jesus was saying. This is the Christ-like humility that is to be exhibited in the daily life of the believer. It is a gift from a covenant-keeping God to the world He created.

INTO ANOTHER DIMENSION

For our part, God is trying to take us into another dimension, and so He is dealing with us about what most hinders us. Our standard in this regard cannot be how we *choose* to live but rather how He has called us to live. Why? Because if we live according to His principles, we will make it through this journey. If not, we may falter along the way.

Life is tough enough as it is; don't make it more so. If someone insists on doing you wrong, show them the love of Christ in return. If they take something from you, offer them something else.

Jesus went so far as to declare:

Give to every man that asketh of thee; and of him that
taketh away thy goods ask them not again.

Verse 30

Whatever people want, give it to them. If they ask for
the shirt off your back, give them your pants too. Why
would you do such a thing? The Bible states plainly:

Therefore if thine enemy hunger, feed him; if he thirst,
give him drink: for in so doing thou shalt heap coals
of fire on his head.   Romans 12:20

Is this a friend you are caring for in this loving way?
No, it's an enemy. So why are you doing it? It is, Jesus
said, to heap coals of fire upon their heads by showing
them the love of Christ in the face of their treachery.

LIFE IS FULL OF ENEMIES

Life is full of enemies. People are hateful and unkind.
They will take advantage of you at every turn. But when
you meet a real Christian, there is an unmistakable genu-
ineness about them. They're different.

But what Jesus said here is hard, isn't it? *"Give to ev-*
ery man that asketh of thee; and of him that taketh away
thy goods ask them not again." You worked hard for those
things, and now they are being taken from you. What
should you do? Jesus said not to ask for that thing back,
just to leave it alone. That's better than trying to fight
over everything. Just leave it with God.

119

Why must you fight for something you already have? If the Lord gave you strength to obtain it in the first place, don't you think He can give you strength to obtain more of it? He said:

> *The LORD is good unto them that wait for him, to the soul that seeketh him.*   Lamentations 3:25

BEING MORE RELAXED

Why are we always in such a hurry? Why are we always so anxious about everything? Why are we always going after things, when the Lord told us just to wait on Him and good things would come to us?

This word *wait* does not indicate inactivity. It doesn't mean to just sit at home waiting for everything to happen. It is an active waiting. We need to get excited because something good is about to happen, and we need to be thanking God in advance of it happening, because it is sure in God. Thank Him even before the answer comes.

GIVING THANKS IN ADVANCE

This is one of the most important reasons we don't receive more from God. We are not actively expecting it, so we don't thank Him enough in advance of its arrival. We wait until it has come because the world has taught us only to give thanks when we have already received a gift.

I give you something, and you say, "Thanks." But isn't it also right to give thanks for the promise of something, even before it comes? It is if you trust the person who made the promise, and, in this case, that person is God Himself.

"That's crazy!" most people would say, but that's Kingdom living, covenant love in our God, giving thanks in advance for all that He has promised.

For example, you might be led to pray, "Thank You, Lord, for a house. I don't know exactly where to look for it, but I want to start thanking You for it in advance, for I know You love me and want me to have it."

I have lived enough years now to have seen many people receive much in life, but I've never seen anything to compare to the blessings that come to those who begin to thank God before they see the answer to their prayers. Waiting to give thanks until you have received the gift is a mistake.

With a person here on earth, it might seem presumptuous to send a thank-you note before receiving their promised gift, but with God it is certainly not. Thank Him in advance, for His love never fails. He will give what He has promised.

OBEYING THE GOLDEN RULE

Jesus then spoke what, by many, has come to be called The Golden Rule:

And as ye would that men should do to you, do ye also to them likewise. Verse 31

Oh, that's a good one! Whatever you would like for other people to do to you is what you need to do to them. *You* start the ball rolling. If you want others to show you love, then you show them love first. Don't wait for them to make the first move; *you* make the first move.

A person might hate you for some reason, but, if every time you pass them by, you smile and tell them how much you love them, they will not be able to resist your love for long. You will eventually win their hearts. Love and true acts of love reach their way down inside of people and move them.

This is the true Christian life. This is covenant living, and it allows you to demonstrate what you have. You cannot give something you don't have in the first place, but if you have the love of God, it will surely be seen in your relationship with others.

You may be thinking, "I'm not there yet." That's okay. At least you recognize your lack. Keep growing until you reach this level. You'll get there.

"SINNERS ALSO LOVE THOSE THAT LOVE THEM"

Jesus went on:

For if ye love them which love you, what thank have ye? for sinners also love those that love them.

Verse 32

This is another of the things we see prevalent in the Church today. Too many Christians only love those who love them back. Why not reach out to those who are seated two pews away and greet them in the love of the Lord? You can notice, in any church you care to attend, that after the service, certain people greet only other certain people. We seem to reach out to the same people we reached out to last week, last month and last year, and yet there are others who need and want our fellowship but have not been able to receive it. If you only love those who love you back, there is no reward in that.

We are in a covenant of Kingdom love, and God's love demands better of us. Even the people of the world, those who don't know God at all, love those who love them back. So we must do more, and we *can* do more. In God's business, we cannot afford to show partiality. We cannot choose to love one and refuse to love another.

GOD GAVE ME A LOVE FOR THIS COUNTRY AND THIS PEOPLE

I'm from Trinidad and I love my country, but it was God's love that compelled me to come here to America and adopt this as my country. I love Americans, and when I'm around any of them, I feel like I fit in like a hand in a glove.

Oh, I can't yet speak like an American (although I've been trying now for more than twenty years). I just can't seem to get it. But that doesn't make me love this country and its people any less.

LET LOVE EXPAND YOUR FRIENDSHIPS

What would it be like if I showed love only to those who showed love to me? Instead, I must reach out to those I've never spoken to before.

There are people you communicate with every single day. You speak with them by phone, send them text messages, leave them voice messages and e-mail messages, and you also greet them warmly at church. What about everyone else you pass on a daily basis? They need your love as well. Let love expand your friendships.

"SINNERS ALSO DO EVEN THE SAME"

And if ye do good to them which do good to you, what thank have ye? for sinners also do even the same.

Verse 33

If the Lord speaks to me to give to someone, I must do it, but not only to those who show kindness to me. I may meet someone during the course of my day who has no idea where their next meal is coming from, and that person needs my help. They may not have ever given anything to me, but that's not the point. I must give to them, expecting nothing in return. This is the love of God in action.

Why should we always give to those who already have? We must look for someone in need and show them God's covenant love.

When God speaks in this way, you must act. Do good to someone you have never done good to before (and someone who has never done good to you). Don't let your motive in giving be expecting some future return from that person. Let your motivation be the pure love of a covenant-keeping God.

WHAT A WONDERFUL THING!

Being a Christian is such a wonderful thing, and I've been experiencing it since I was a teenager and gave my life to Jesus. God has been so good to me and shown me so much mercy and favor that I would never think of turning back to a life of sin. Instead, I try to obey the scriptural admonition:

> *Therefore, my beloved brethren, be ye stedfast, un-moveable, always abounding in the work of the Lord, forasmuch as ye know that your labour is not in vain in the Lord.*   1 Corinthians 15:58

I know that my labor is not in vain, and I must do acts of love because the Lord has loved me and done so much for me. I remember the days someone came to me and placed an envelope with a large sum of money in it into my pocket, when I had done nothing to deserve it. I didn't even realize what they had done until a day or so later when I looked in the envelope. How surprised I was to find thousands of dollars there!

How grateful I was! God was demonstrating His love to me in ways I had never thought possible. We, in turn, must begin to demonstrate His love to others as never before. This will bring unsaved men to Christ and lift up and encourage those who are already saved.

"SINNERS ALSO LEND TO SINNERS"

Jesus continued:

And if ye lend to them of whom ye hope to receive, what thank have ye? for sinners also lend to sinners, to receive as much again.   Verses 34

If sinners do this, then we Christians must live by an even higher standard.

I know what it is to lend money and never have it returned. So what did I do? I just gave it to the Lord. As the old saying goes, "Why weep over spilt milk?"

When a genuine believer loves you, they will do anything for you, and when the love of God sweeps over our hearts as a church body, then all of the needs of those present will be met. There will be no lack among us. No one will go away wondering how they will go on existing the next day. God is able to meet every need among us, and He does it through expressions of His Kingdom love.

"LOVE YOUR ENEMIES"

Now Jesus got down to the most difficult point:

JESUS' STUNNING CONCLUSIONS ON LOVE

But love ye your enemies, and do good, and lend, hoping for nothing again; and your reward shall be great, and ye shall be the children of the Highest: for he is kind unto the unthankful and to the evil. Verse 35

When you can love your enemies, what happens? Suddenly people know you are God's child (see the next chapter for more details on this important subject). This pleases God, and He will reward you openly for it.

Personally, I don't have time to focus on enemies. I'm so busy doing the work of the Lord, I couldn't tell you if I have enemies or not and, if so, where they are or what they're doing at the moment. That's not my focus. You may have time to think about, comment about or worry about what someone has said about you, but I just don't. To me, that's very childish. I'm busy looking at the bigger picture, and in the process, I'm loving everyone, and Jesus said my reward would be great.

Oh, I like that! If you have so much time on your hands that you can focus on who is your current enemy and what they might or might not be saying about you, then you need to find a corner in God's harvest field and get busy reaping it for His glory. Serving God and others in love will cause you to forget the efforts of your opposers. Just forget every enemy. God is able to make His grace *"abound toward you"*:

And God is able to make all grace abound toward you; that ye, always having all sufficiency in all things, may abound to every good work. 2 Corinthians 9:8

127

"BE YE THEREFORE MERCIFUL"

Jesus went on:

Be ye therefore merciful, as your Father also is merciful. Verse 36

Have mercy on others, just as God has had mercy on you. Don't be so arrogant and hard on others, as if you were already perfect yourself. How can you afford to be so harsh with others when you need mercy yourself?

Who made you the judge anyway? Put your gavel down and show mercy to your fellowman.

Many are quick to slam down their gavel and declare a guilty verdict, but you can't afford to do that. You need mercy yourself. Show the love of God (and that means showing mercy), and people will want to come to you for help and be part of what you're doing. If all you can offer others is your judgment, they will run the other way. Draw them by your love. This is all part of God's Kingdom covenant love.

CONFRONTED BY A MASTER OF THE LAW

One day Jesus was confronted by a master of the Law:

And, behold, a certain lawyer stood up, and tempted him, saying, Master, what shall I do to inherit eternal life?

128

He said unto him, What is written in the law? how readest thou?

And he answering said, Thou shalt love the Lord thy God with all thy heart, and with all thy soul, and with all thy strength, and with all thy mind; and thy neighbour as thyself.

And he said unto him, Thou hast answered right: this do, and thou shalt live.   Luke 10:25-28

Many of us don't even love ourselves, and that is where the love of others begins. If you love yourself, you will treat others as they deserve to be treated.

REMEMBER HOW YOU GOT TO WHERE YOU ARE TODAY

When tempted to judge those who are not on the same spiritual level with us, let us remember how we got to where we are today and what we were like before we got there. We were worse than some of those we are now judging so harshly. There was a time when you were in the nightclub dancing the potato, and while you did that, you were snorting some illegal substance and drinking way too much liquor. So how is it that you are now suddenly turning on others who do the same things or even something less offensive? What kind of love is that?

Some people hate smoking so badly that anytime someone passes them who smells of cigarettes, they are mumbling under their breath, rebuking the person and their bad habit. This is probably because they had the same bad habit themselves before they were saved. What should you do? Just pray for those who have bad habits. That's the best thing you can do. Yes, they stink, but you used to smell worse than that. So just keep praying for them.

DON'T DRIVE THEM AWAY

"Save them, Jesus!" should be our prayer. If you continually condemn people who do things you don't like, you'll just drive them further away from the Lord and the Church. Instead of heaping coals of fire upon their heads, through showing them the love of Christ, we too often heap condemnation and scorn on them and push them away. Stop being so judgmental and start showing mercy, and I guarantee you will see more souls coming into the Kingdom of God.

Because people are doing things you don't approve of, you get judgmental and start rebuking the devil in them, and they sense that attitude and are repelled.

OUR ATTITUDE IS HYPOCRITICAL

Jesus showed us the hypocrisy of our judgmental attitudes:

And why beholdest thou the mote that is in thy brother's eye, but considerest not the beam that is in thine own eye? Or how wilt thou say to thy brother, Let me pull out the mote out of thine eye; and, behold, a beam

is in thine own eye? Thou hypocrite, first cast out the
beam out of thine own eye; and then shalt thou see
clearly to cast out the mote out of thy brother's eye.

Matthew 7:3-5

We might compare this *"mote"* which is in your brother's eye to a 2 X 4 and the *"beam"* that is in your own eye to an 8 X 8 post. Which is more serious? And yet we concentrate on what is affecting our brother and ignore what is affecting us. That's not love.

We're like a bunch of monkeys, making fun of each other, when we all look about the same. Take inventory today. Is God's love filling your heart and influencing how you view an react to others?

Always remember: The love of God is "rich and free." It's "measureless and strong." "It reaches to the highest star," but still can extend "to the lowest hell." God has extended His love to you. Now you must extend His love through you to others.

Why not start today? Begin *Discovering the Untapped Power of Covenant.*

Chapter 16

LOVE AS A UNIQUE IDENTIFIER

Ye shall know them by their fruits. Do men gather grapes of thorns, or figs of thistles? Even so every good tree bringeth forth good fruit; but a corrupt tree bringeth forth evil fruit. A good tree cannot bring forth evil fruit, neither can a corrupt tree bring forth good fruit. Every tree that bringeth not forth good fruit is hewn down, and cast into the fire. Wherefore by their fruits ye shall know them.   Matthew 7:16-20

A new commandment I give unto you, That ye love one another; as I have loved you, that ye also love one another. By this shall all men know that ye are my disciples, if ye have love one to another.

Matthew 7:16-20

John 13:34-35

The most distinguishing mark of a Christian should be his or her love, a love emanating from God Himself.

133

So we Christians should have love like no one else on the Earth. These passages are the words of Jesus Himself, not that of any man, and He named love as the unique identifier of His children.

YOU CAN RECOGNIZE A TREE BY WHAT IS ON IT

You can recognize a tree by what is on it. If you see a peach hanging on a tree, you would never make the mistake of calling that a lime tree. You know what it is by what it bears. If it has peaches on it, then it's a peach tree.

If a tree has apples on it, you would never call it a pear tree. You know that it has to be an apple tree because it has apples on it. In the very same way, Christians need to bear the fruit of love. Otherwise, something is wrong with the tree.

Sometimes we can go beyond love, but if we don't start with love, which must be the root, or foundation, of every believer, we have to wonder about the authenticity of the tree, the authenticity of the individual experience.

LIFE THROWS MANY THINGS OUR WAY

When we talk about walking in this Kingdom or covenant love, there are many things you must take into account. We have to face many things in life, and often we are not well enough prepared for them, so that our reaction is not always the best. It's time for those of us who call ourselves Christians to recognize our true potential in God's love and to go forth exhibiting that love in our daily lives, whatever happens to come our way, whatever other people do to us or say to us.

This is the way all men will know that we are Christ's disciples: not by how much we know, but by how much we love.

LOVE IS MORE THAN WORDS

True loves is more than words. As noted in an earlier chapter, when a genuine believer loves you, they will do anything for you, and when the love of God sweeps over our hearts as a church body, then all of the needs of those present will be met, and there will be no lack among us. God is able to meet every need among us, and He does it through the manifestation of His love through us.

If you fall deeply in love with Jesus, the members of your family, your neighbors and your entire community will know it very quickly. Even your dog will see the change in you. And if there is no change, then examine your life.

As we noted in the previous chapter, loving those who don't love you is never easy, and we cannot do it in ourselves. Showing mercy to people when we feel they don't deserve mercy is really beyond us. But the world is looking for a demonstration of Kingdom, or covenant, love, and you are the person God has chosen to demonstrate that covenant love to others.

I AM ABLE TO LOVE THEM ANYWAY

I can say that when I know someone doesn't wish me well, I am able to love them anyway. It's not because I am somehow different than others. It's because "the love of God is rich and pure, it's measureless and strong. It goes beyond the highest star and reaches to the lowest hell." Love reaches down in the gutter, where nobody else wants to go, and it compels men and women to come to Christ.

We cannot emphasize it too much: we are known by the love we have for one another. When people see it, they will know you are Christ's disciple. If it's not there, they will wonder if you are a true Christian or not.

So what about you? Why not begin today *Discovering the Untapped Power of Covenant?*

Chapter 17

LOVE: WORDS VS. DEEDS

If ye love me, keep my commandments.

John 14:15

Because love covers a multitude of sins, it is the most powerful force in the world. So we, as members of the Church of the Lord Jesus Christ, must learn to love the unreached and also to love one another. This is a new commandment given unto us by Jesus Himself, that we love each other, even as He loved us. It is this that will enable you to convince the world that Christ is in you.

SOME GO OVERBOARD

I know that some go overboard in this matter of love (for example, walking down the street, saying "I love you" to everyone they meet). But love is far more than words.

It is a demonstration, an outworking of something you feel deep inside, and it is planted there by God Himself.

You can demonstrate love in many different ways. For instance, you can be stern with someone who needs it, and that will be a loving gesture. If that's what they need, then that's what love demands. Love knows what is needed at the moment and responds to it.

A DEMONSTRATION OF LOVE ALSO INCLUDES WORDS

But don't get me wrong. A demonstration of love also includes words. Most of us married folk don't tell our spouses nearly enough that we love them. Say it, and then demonstrate it with your actions.

The problem with the words of love is that we can say them when the love is not really there. As the saying goes, "Words are cheap; actions cost a lot more." The solution is: Say it and then back it up with your deeds.

Children are keen. If we love them, they know it. If you just say you love them and then are not kind to them when they need your kindness, they know the truth about your love (or lack of love, in this case).

YOU CAN'T FOOL GOD

Our Lord also cannot be fooled in this regard. If we love Him, He knows it, and if we don't, then He knows that too. My love is spoken to Him, but, even more so, it is demonstrated to Him in my obedience to His Word on a daily basis. He said: *"If ye love me, keep my commandments."*

What are some specific commandments that I can keep that will demonstrate my love to the Lord? Well, for instance, this one:

Not forsaking the assembling of ourselves together, as the manner of some is; but exhorting one another: and so much the more, as ye see the day approaching.
Hebrews 10:25

When it is time to worship God and study His Word, I want to be in church because I have fallen in love with Jesus and don't ever want to be away from His presence. Going to His house shows Him how much I care.

Do you remember your courting days? For those of us who are older, there were no cell phones and no texting, so we had to find a phone and dial our loved one. But, whatever it took, every single day we wanted to talk to each other because we were so in love.

I don't know about you, but I had a specific time when I would try to call my intended, and as that time approached, I began to get excited.

When was the last time we felt that kind of excitement about attending the House of God and worshipping Him? Whenever we call upon Him, He hears us, and He will answer. That should excite us and bring us regularly to His house.

I SET ASIDE TIME FOR GOD

When anyone tries to call me on Sunday morning, they find that I don't answer my phone. I have a sacred appointment with God that day, and I try not to allow anything to interrupt that appointment. Each Saturday evening, I set aside time to talk to the Lord about His will for our Sunday services, so again, I don't answer my phone, and my wife has to tell anyone who calls that I'm not available. That time is reserved for God. He deserves that.

LOVING THE HOUSE OF GOD

I love to be in the House of God and, for me, it's too long from Sunday to Wednesday, and from Sunday to Sunday seems like an eternity. Often, on Wednesday evenings, I am tired from the work of the day, but I want to be in the House of God anyway. Later, after we have studied God's Word together, I feel strengthened. His love empowers me, so how can I not show Him my love in this way?

Refuse to allow anything to pull you away from God and His love, and insist on showing Him and others love, in word and in deed.

Are you ready to get started? Begin today *Discovering the Untapped Power of Covenant.*

Chapter 18
WHAT TRUE LOVE IS NOT

Charity [love] seeketh not her own.

1 Corinthians 13:5

Far too many people in our modern world equate love with sex. Sex is wonderful, when it's done right, but we must be clear: all the shacking up, loose living and wrong living that is going on today is not love in any sense of the word. It is nothing more than lust trying to glorify itself by another name.

LUST HARMS ITS VICTIMS

Lust is always desirous of getting something at the expense of others. A young man looks at a young woman, and suddenly he's like a dog in heat. He goes after her with one thing on his mind. He is determined to get her into bed. And yet, for some reason, we call that "love." It's clearly not love. Soon after he finally gets her into bed, he walks away, looking for someone else he might prey upon.

Can I prove all this by the Word of God? someone might ask. Oh, yes, I can.

AMNON'S LUST LED TO TRAGEDY

For instance, in Old Testament times, there was a young girl by the name of Tamar, and she had a half-brother named Amnon. They were children of King David.

Just think about that! Lust even gets into families and seeks to mess them up, and if you flirt with this terrible monster, it will trail you relentlessly until it gets it's evil way.

Amnon so lusted for his sister that it made him physically ill. Lust, this desire to have your physical gratification, is so strong that it makes you do crazy things.

WHAT TERRIBLE LIES!

When David heard about Amnon's sickness, he went to visit him. Rather than confess his evil desire, Amnon took advantage of the opportunity to ask if his sister Tamar could make him one of her special cakes and bring it to him. He felt that would make him feel so much better.

What terrible lies! This young man had no desire for cakes. All he wanted was to bed his innocent and virgin sister.

David did not sense what was afoot. Who could have imagined the terrible thing that was in this young man's heart? So Amnon's request was granted, and Tamar was called upon to make special cakes and bring them to him. How terrible it was for both of them that when she had come, lust so consumed Amnon that he rose up and violated his little sister.

THAT'S WHAT LUST IS LIKE

Can you imagine such a thing? Oh, yes. That's exactly what lust is like. To Amnon, having a sexual encounter with his virgin sister was sweeter than cake. And yet, once he had consummated the thing, he despised her. He threw her out the door and slammed it in her face, as if the whole affair had somehow been her fault.

That's what lust will do. Guard yourselves, saints, against this evil that has so overwhelmed the people of our modern day.

TRUE LOVE IS JUST THE OPPOSITE OF LUST

In contrast to lust, love always desires to give to others. Do you know one of those people who often invite you out to dine with them, but they seem to always forget their wallet, and you end up having to pay the bill? Does it make you suspicious of their "love"? When someone has an ulterior or selfish motive in everything they do, that's not love. Love is unselfish.

Love, like a blanket, covers, and one thing it covers is a *"multitude of sins"*:

> *And above all things have fervent charity among yourselves: for charity shall cover the multitude of sins.* 1 Peter 4:8

Our heavenly Father is our example in this. Regardless of what we have done, when we come to Him in true repentance, He loves us, receives us and covers our sins.

There is nothing to compare with a person who is full of the love of God. That love is measureless, it is rich and it is strong. It goes beyond the highest star and reaches to the lowest Hell. As noted earlier, no dictionary could adequately describe this word *love,* and a few chapters in a book cannot do it justice. It must be lived out in our everyday lives.

GOD STARTED IT ALL

Again, God is our example in love. He so loved the world, that He gave His only Son. Love was what was missing under the old covenant, so that should be the hallmark of the Church today and the mark of each of us who are members of that Church.

You cannot come to God unless His love compels you, and once you are His, that same love begins to manifest through you, causing you to love even those who despitefully use you. As Christians, we can love the unlovable, and if we are covenant-keeping people, there should be no hate in us whatsoever for anyone and no false love or lust, only the purity of God's love.

What about you? Is God's love filling your being? If not, begin today *Discovering the Untapped Power of Covenant.*

Chapter 19

MATURING IN LOVE

But speaking the truth in love, may grow up into him in all things, which is the head, even Christ.

Ephesians 4:15

All of us are at different spiritual levels. Of necessity, we have the babes in Christ, those just starting out. Although they may be the same physical size as others, they still carry a pacifier in their mouths, and they require a lot of attention.

THE CARNAL STAGE

Then we have the carnal and unspiritual Christians. These are just coming out of the baby stage, and they desperately want to move on to maturity. But they are moving a little too fast for their own good, so they make a lot of mistakes. Just as in the process of human development, moving gradually into the area of spiritual maturity produces the best results. It is a process that takes time, and it cannot be rushed.

Watch the person who tries to move too fast, for *carnal* describes them well. Sometimes they are in, and sometimes they are out. Sometimes they feel high, and sometimes they feel low. They ride the elevator of life. On Sunday they are at the highest peak, but on Monday morning, they are often back in the basement level.

I'm afraid this describes many Christians today, and if it describes you, it's time to move out of your carnality and onto a level of strength in Christ. Then the events of daily life will not send you reeling into depression and despair.

BE STRONG IN THE LORD

The Scriptures set a standard for us:

Finally, my brethren, be strong in the Lord, and in the power of his might. Put on the whole armour of God, that ye may be able to stand against the wiles of the devil. Ephesians 6:10-11

The apostle Paul was able to personally declare:

But none of these things move me, neither count I my life dear unto myself, so that I might finish my course with joy, and the ministry, which I have received of the Lord Jesus, to testify the gospel of the grace of God. Acts 20:24

Carnal Christians are led by their emotions and their own will and not by the Spirit of God. "I don't feel like going to church today," they may say, so they simply don't go. "I don't feel like talking to anyone today," they might say, so they don't. This is operating in the flesh. Immature people may have high aspirations, but something is always holding them back. If that describes you, then this can be your day of deliverance. God can and will bring you up to a higher level of living, covenant love.

CARNAL JUST MEANS IMMATURE

When we call someone carnal, we're not necessarily saying something bad about them. We're just describing where they happen to live at the moment in their level of maturity (or lack thereof).

Sometimes they don't even recognize their lack. They think they're doing just fine. Back in Trinidad, we called such people "wishy-washy." You're not sure if they're coming or going, and they seem to flow downstream with the current rather than push their way upstream.

It requires no energy at all for a fish to flow with the current, but to move upstream takes some stamina. You must come against the things that oppose and hinder you and force your way forward against the current.

Some people get offended over every little thing. They are sure that nobody loves them, and they are desperately in search of love. But today I want to declare that we are part of a covenant of love. Search no more. God loves you, and He has called you to love others.

THE THIRD STAGE: A MATURE CHRISTIAN

The third and final stage of the believer is that of a mature Christian. This is a person who has passed through dangers, toils and snares, and yet always keeps going. The grace that has brought them safe thus far will surely lead them on. These are strong believers, and when the enemy attempts to turn them aside, they face him head-on and say, "Go ahead, devil. Take your best shot. See if you can move me." That's God's love in action.

One night, many years ago, I was preaching in a large open-air crusade, and I publicly declared, "Devil, this is my current address (and I gave it). Come and get me if you think you can." The next night he was waiting for me. We had some six hundred people packed into a public park that night for an evangelistic meeting, and the devil showed his ugly face.

A man who was full of demons came forward for prayer. When I laid hands on him to begin to pray, he reached out and ripped one of the pockets off of my jacket. When I tried laying hands on him again, he ripped off the other pocket. By the time I finished with him, half of my jacket was ripped away, and I went home that night in rags.

THE WORST PART

The worst part was that, before the man could be completely free, he ran off into the nearby fields. So, when you tell the devil your telephone number and zip code, you'd better have the goods. He's coming after you, and that's the reason you cannot afford to remain a babe in Christ or a carnal Christian who is always confused or perplexed. Move on up into the maturity of God's love.

HOW CAN YOU DO IT?

How can you do that? First, you must be determined in your heart that you are tired of constantly dealing with the flesh. If you're satisfied to live on that level, that's where you'll remain. If your mind is made up and you're determined to move on up, then you will.

When this is the case, the enemy will find no place in you. When he tries, he will find that there is no vacancy. You're all filled up with God and His love, and there's no room for the devil.

Oh, I like that. Tell the devil today: "Devil, I'm all filled up, and so there's no vacancy, no place for you, in my life." When he hears that, he'll have to flee.

I remember going around one town looking for a place to stay, and the sign in front of every hotel read NO VACANCY. For a while I thought I was going to have to spend the night in the car. Thankfully, far down the street I spotted a sign that said VACANCY. I was so happy to see that sign.

As Christians, we should have our NO VACANCY sign out for Satan. There should be room in us only for the things of God and His covenant love. If He's dealing with you about your need in this regard, let Him have His way today.

STILL IN THE FIRST GRADE

Some of us are still in the first grade, and we have a long way to go, but that's okay. You have to start somewhere. Just be sure you don't stay in the first grade forever. That would be sad, and it's not what God wants for you.

If you've reached second grade, give thanks, but don't stop there. There is so much more to have in God. Stick with it and you'll reach the sixth grade and keep going.

But be careful! Don't try to jump from first to sixth. That doesn't work. You need to pass through all the stages of growth to get to where God has called you to be in His Kingdom love.

HE SHOULD HAVE KNOWN BETTER

How many times have we heard people say, "He should have known better!" But they're often wrong about that. We can only operate on the level we have attained. You are in a certain stage of Christian life, and that's all that can be expected of you. So put down your hammer and begin to show mercy to your brothers and sisters. You might think they should know better, but they only know what they know—nothing more. If this is not true, why do the Scriptures say to us so forcefully (as we noted in an earlier chapter) that we should "bear the infirmities of the weak"?

If we don't learn this lesson, Christianity is doomed to extinction, for no man alive can attain to perfection overnight. We all go through the same growing process.

The strong, for some reason, only want to deal with other strong people, and if someone falls short of their ideals, they put them down, conveniently forgetting that they were not always strong themselves. What happened with going to the weak and offering them your help? That person doesn't need your condemnation; they are condemned enough already. What they need is to hear that you love them and are praying for them. They need to hear you say, "You can make it, and I will help you."

STEP BY STEP

God wants to take each and every one of us step by step until we have reached a place of excellence. His will for our lives is something we can reach, but to do so we must continue in His Word and continue growing in His love and the manifestation of that love to others.

What is your decision today. Why not say Yes to God and start *Discovering the Untapped Power of Covenant.*

Part V

AGREEMENT WITH MEN

Chapter 20

SEEKING THE RIGHT KIND OF AGREEMENT

Again I say unto you, That if two of you shall agree
on earth as touching any thing that they shall ask,
it shall be done for them of my Father which is in
heaven.   Matthew 18:19

Agreement is powerful. So what does this mean to us today on a practical level? When God speaks to us to do something great, we often just launch out, expecting everything to happen as He has said, and too often we are disappointed. Why?

SEEKING AGREEMENT AMONG OUR BROTHERS

When we feel called to do something, it is always best to first seek someone of like mind to join with you in prayer about the matter and help you know what direction to take, how to take it and with whom to take it. When you just jump into the water and begin swimming on your own, too often you get nowhere. Or worse, you *can* drown.

Find someone who can agree with you in everything important in life. God's promise is that if two of us on Earth agree on something, it will be done by Him in Heaven. So why exhaust yourself trying to do everything on your own, when strength and victory come through agreement?

There is much more teaching in God's Word on this important subject, but it is beyond the scope of this book. Suffice it to say that there are many things we might accomplish in life if we would only join forces with others to see it happen.

WE DON'T EVEN KNOW

Too often we don't even know that someone has a vision or is trying to do something until we hear about their failure. We're surprised because that's the first we have known of it.

I can't tell you how many times someone has come to me and said, "Pastor, will you please pray for me?"

"What's going on?" I ask.

"Well, I tried such and such, and it didn't work."

But that was the first I had heard of it. I knew nothing until that moment, so they were trying to achieve it entirely on their own, without the help of their fellow believers (or even their principle spiritual leaders). This is not good. Why risk facing every enemy alone, when God has given you others to stand by your side?

"Why didn't you come before," I ask, "and let us touch and agree? That's how the covenant blessing falls."

But by then, it is often too late. When you find someone who will stand with you on a particular subject of desire, God promises victory, so take the time and make the effort to find them.

Whatever you are doing, it only makes sense to consult others who might have some experience with that particular area of life and can also join their faith to yours. And it goes without saying that whatever you do, never start something without first consulting God first.

STANDING WITH EACH OTHER

There are other covenant matters that we can do for each other. For instance, we should be able to say to our fellow brothers and sisters:

"If I hear something bad about you, I will not repeat it. Instead, I will pray for you every day."

"If I have nothing good to say about you, I will say nothing at all."

"I will not stand by as others say bad things about you."

"In all of your struggles and disappointments, I will not pull you down further. Rather, I will do everything I can to lift you up and help you to stand."

"My desire for you is that God bless you in every way and put you on top."

That's covenant with your fellow believers, and the Scriptures promise: "if *two of you shall agree on earth as touching any thing that they shall ask, it shall be done for them of my Father which is in heaven.*" That's powerful!

WE MAY NEVER AGREE ON EVERYTHING

There are certain things we might never be able to agree on. One day I noticed that the skies had turned black, and rain was about to come, and I had work I needed to get done. I turned to my wife and asked her to agree with me that the rain would pass over. "But we need rain," she objected. And that illustrates the problem.

We cannot agree on everything, but when we can agree on what needs to be done, touch your fellow believer and speak your agreement out loud, and Heaven will take notice. That's God's promise and that's the power of covenant.

When your neighbor is having a hard time, touch them and say these simple words, "Neighbor, we can make it, no matter how tough the times may be." Those simple words will have a powerful effect.

LIVE IN COVENANT
WITH ONE ANOTHER

God is calling on the members of His Church to live in covenant, not only with Him, but with one another. He will give us memories to retain the laws He has written on our hearts and courage to put them into practice, to be a blessing to all those around us.

When God does something, He does it well, and He does it completely, and there is no limit to what He will do in and through us, as individuals and as a body. For too long, however, we have limited God by our lack of faith, and therefore His hands have been tied in many of the situations we face in life as His representatives. Let us break free from all that hinders us and hold each other up, as we go forward together.

Agreement is so powerful that when our politicians decide to pray together, instead of working to bring each other down, something wonderful will happen in this nation. Some may think this is going over the line, but why not go over the line? What do we have to lose?

I promise that this kind of right agreement will work for you and enable you to achieve your destiny. Why not try it? Start today *Discovering the Untapped Power of Covenant?*

Chapter 21

AVOIDING THE WRONG KIND OF AGREEMENT

And when the inhabitants of Gibeon heard what Joshua had done unto Jericho and to Ai, they did work wilily, and went and made as if they had been ambassadors, and took old sacks upon their asses, and wine bottles, old, and rent, and bound up; and old shoes and clouted upon their feet, and old garments upon them; and all the bread of their provision was dry and mouldy. And they went to Joshua unto the camp at Gilgal, and said unto him, and to the men of Israel, We be come from a far country: now therefore make ye a league [or covenant] with us.   Joshua 9:3-6

In the days of Joshua, in the critical period when the the people of Israel were retaking the Promised Land, they suffered a terrible defeat one day because they made a covenant with the wrong people.

163

THE FORCES OF DECEIT

Suddenly, that day what appeared to be a small group of representatives from a far nation came to meet with the leaders of Israel. The men were all wearing what appeared to be very old and worn clothes and shoes, and they carried what appeared to be very old and stale provisions. They said they had made a long journey, and they were desirous of entering into a peace pact with Israel.

Sadly, the men of Israel fell for this tale. In truth, these men were from a nearby tribe that hated God and His people and wanted to wipe them off the face of the earth. They knew that if Israel's leaders could be deceived into making a peace pact with them, they would not be able to break it, and the lives of these enemies would be spared.

An agreement, or covenant, is so powerful that you must be careful who you make one with. A covenant with the wrong people can do you irreparable harm, so this is a matter of life and death.

GOING BY WHAT YOU SEE

The leaders of Israel went by what they saw that day. There was mold on the bread these men carried, their meat was spoiling, and their appearance was that of paupers. In reality, the men were rich and had done all of this on purpose to fool God's people. It worked, and Israel suffered the consequences of this deceit for years to come. Join yourself in covenant with the wrong people, and you will find yourself in a heap of trouble.

Since agreement is powerful, we must make the right agreement. If we make a wrong decision in this regard, we will learn about it eventually, but by then it may be too late. Don't gain wisdom in this way. Get it from God now, and make right decisions about who you agree with in this life.

When we realize that decisions have consequences, we become more careful about consulting God and the elders among us before making them. If there is no one nearby we can consult with, we may need to make a long-distance phone call. In my case, when I need advice I call ministers I know and respect, and I find their counsel to be invaluable.

DIVINE WISDOM IS NEEDED IN DATING

Dating may seem to be a very different subject, but in reality it's not. When you date someone, you are entering into agreement with that person. This is an especially dangerous game because emotions are involved. The person you are attracted to may be beautiful (or handsome), and because you are lonely and desperate for companionship, you fall for them quickly, without getting to know them well and without seeking the wise counsel of others.

"But I love her," men say, or "I love him," in the case of the lady. A future with this person looks very good to him or her (or both) at that moment, and just days later they may suddenly announce their intention to marry.

If they are young, they may have no idea what marriage is all about. They have consulted no one and are only being carried along by the excitement of their infatuation. They cannot imagine anything that would intrude upon their current happiness, and so they cannot imagine living without this person by their side.

They are so "in love" that they can't sleep at night, and they have no appetite for food. Their every thought is consumed with the desire for that person's companionship. So what happens? They quickly marry, over the objections of anyone and everyone around them. It's their life, and they know what they want and what they are sure will bring them happiness. So they don't welcome any outside "interference."

THE PROBLEM

The problem is that they don't really know what they're getting themselves into, and they don't realize how serious it is to enter into covenant with someone they don't know well. All too often the result is that this person is headed for marital problems and much personal grief. This could all have been avoided if they had been willing to consult the Lord and His faithful people.

When others try to give you advice, they're not trying to interfere in your personal matters or hinder your future happiness. They're trying to save you the heartache that comes by being in covenant with the wrong person. This person may look good and seem appealing, but when you really get to know them, do they have the same heart as you? Do you really agree with you on the important issues of life? You have to know for sure.

GOD SAID "WAIT"!

Never rush into these things. God said: "WAIT!":

But they that wait upon the LORD shall renew their strength; they shall mount up with wings as eagles; they shall run, and not be weary; and they shall walk, and not faint. ⸱ Isaiah 40:31

To *wait* involves more than marking time. It denotes a time of careful observation. It is not a time of doing nothing. You ARE doing something (something very important) even as you wait.

The promises for those who wait are awesome:

They ... shall renew their strength.
They shall mount up with wings as eagles.
They shall run, and not be weary.
They shall walk, and not faint.

These are the rewards of waiting on the Lord and not rushing ahead with your own plans in any endeavor in life. Oh, that more people would understand these basic principles. It would spare them so much grief.

PRESSURED TO LEAVE THE CHURCH

I was preaching once in a church in Denver, Colorado, and I met a young lady who had been attending the church for about a year. She had become very active in the church and was already part of the choir. But when she began dating a young man, he turned out to be of another religion, and he soon began pressuring her to leave the church.

She was part of a group that went out to a restaurant that night with the pastor, and I was invited to go along. Seated next to her, I confided: "I don't know you, Sister, but I sense that something is awfully wrong in your life right now. What's going on with you?"

Her sister jumped up and said, "She's dating a person of another religion! That's what's going on!"

I was stunned by that revelation, "You must know," I reminded her, "that darkness and light don't mix. You should know better than that." But when it comes to dating (and many other things in life) we don't seem to know better. Our emotions get the best of us, and we make foolish decisions.

MEN OFTEN FOOL WOMEN

We all know men who have fooled women by flashing their check books, when, in reality, they had nothing at all in the bank. They were driving beautiful cars, but they turned out to be borrowed. They had on the most beautiful shoes, and they were not even theirs. Before long, they had the woman saying, "Oh, he's such a wonderful person. I think I'm in love with him."

They never bothered to pray about it. What's to pray about? He's so polite. He's so generous. He's so caring. He's so giving. In the end she learns, much to her sorrow and surprise, that he's a crook and has done the same thing to other women before her.

Every woman would like to have a decent, upright, good looking man, and men know that. So they say what they know you want to hear, and they do what they know you want to see them do ... at least until they get you, and then the real person slowly begins to emerge. They can't hide the truth forever, but by then it is often too late, and the damage has already been done.

Men know how to mask their weaknesses and make themselves look good to you, long enough to get you. So beware!

IT HAPPENED TO A PROPHETESS IN TRINIDAD

A young lady in our church in Trinidad became a prophetess and preacher of the Word of God, but I'll never forget the night we spoke in a meeting there.

"Pastor," she said, "I have fallen in love with a young man in America. He is working on a visa for me to go and join him there."

"Is he saved?" I asked. That's always the first question because it's central to everything else.

"Well, not yet," she answered, "but almost. Any day now he'll be saved. He just *has* to get saved because he's such a sweet and caring person."

I could see that she had fallen head over heels in love with him, and I sensed that it was a trick of the enemy to take her away from the church and the ministry. "Look," I said very frankly. "You can't go this route. That's all there is to it. This is a trick, and if you do this thing, you will suffer the consequences." Thank God she took that advice and continues serving the Lord today. That man was nothing more than a wolf in sheep's clothing.

SAMSON'S FATAL CHOICE

Men are often fooled too. Like Samson, many men are desperate for a wife, and Delilah looks good to them. Never mind that she can't sew, she can't cook, and she hates housework. They want Delilah, for they are sure she will please them well.

In the end, it was this very Delilah who caused Samson the loss of his wonderful position and eventually caused his death. Don't make another move without seeking God's will on this all-important subject.

EVEN PASTORS ARE GUILTY

Even pastors are guilty of judging by the exterior and not seeking God enough when it comes to people. Not too long ago, a lady told me about a young man she met, and he became interested in her. He had never been to church in his life, but because she refused to play loose with him, he pretended to be intrigued with her faith and went to her church. When he asked the pastor if he could join the church, he was immediately taken in as a new member.

This infuriated the woman. She went to the pastor and said, "That man is a crook. He has never been saved or baptized, and yet you took him in as a member in good standing. You didn't ask him any questions or demand anything of him. And all he wanted was to get close to me. This is not the kind of church I want to be part of." And she went in search of a better church to attend.

We have people today who are in church on Sunday, and the rest of the week they are out peddling drugs and promoting prostitution, and these are very abusive people, verbally and physically. As a pastor, you have to see how people are walking in their everyday life, not just what they say on Sunday morning.

As an aside: women who are being abused should report it, to their pastors and to local officials. There is no excuse for that type of behavior, and it should be dealt with very severely and decisively. Don't let anyone make you a punching bag. Covenant or no covenant, men who do such things have to be straightened out.

SURROUNDED BY ENEMIES

This whole episode with Joshua had started in the following way:

171

And it came to pass, when all the kings which were on this side Jordan, in the hills, and in the valleys, and in all the coasts of the great sea over against Lebanon, the Hittite, and the Amorite, the Canaanite, the Perizzite, the Hivite, and the Jebusite, heard thereof; that they gathered themselves together, to fight with Joshua and with Israel, with one accord.   Joshua 9:1-2

Can you imagine what it was like to have so many nations joining to fight against you? Maybe you can, because when you take a stand for God, spiritual forces close ranks against you. Discouragement, confusion, perplexity, strife and torment all seem to come at you at once from every direction.

Why does this happen? Because the devil and his forces don't want to see you doing well and doing right. You were on their side so long that the loss of your services pains them. Because they hate God, they also hate anyone who aligns themselves with God. And that means you.

What evil had Joshua done to all of these people? None! They just hated him because he was successful and prosperous and loved and served Jehovah God and because God had given the people of Israel victory over the cities of Jericho and Ai.

ARMIES MAKE PACTS, OR COVENANTS

Armies that joined forces to fight like these did always made a pact, another type of covenant. In this case, it was a covenant for wrongdoing. As a sign of their agreement to fight together, they beat their swords against their shields, and this notified the armies they were about to face that agreement had been reached, and they would soon be facing a unified front.

It was in this terrifying moment that the Gibeonite men came riding up on their donkeys, looking very much like they had made a long journey to get there, and the men of Israel were deceived.

How clever these enemies were! They came very respectfully and totally misrepresenting who they were and what their intentions were, they publicly recognized the greatness of Israel's God and expressed a desire to align themselves with this people. It all sounded so very good. And that's exactly why we have to be so very careful.

WOLVES COMING IN

Some years ago, I was pastoring the fastest growing church in a certain community. Every week we were taking in fifteen or twenty new members, and they were coming from every direction. Other pastors and Christian leaders were aligning themselves with us, and our youth group was exploding. In the midst of all that excitement, a certain young man slipped into the congregation unnoticed. When he finally came to our attention, he seemed to everyone to be a brilliant and talented person, and he began working his way up, until he eventually held a very responsible position with the youth department of the church.

Six or seven months went by before I noticed anything wrong. Then some of our people began showing up late for service or not coming at all. My Youth President came to me and said that he had decided to take a month off. "I'm very tired, and I just need some rest," he told me. "I want to seek the Lord."

That seemed very strange to me. He was only nineteen years old. "You're not an old man," I said. "What's going on?" He had been so faithful that he often came by and cut my lawn for me, and he washed my car every Saturday. He was reluctant now to say what was on his mind, but we eventually learned that the other young man (whom everyone had considered to be so brilliant and talented) held a doctrine very different from the doctrine of our church. He had loaned tape recordings to the Youth President of teachings on his doctrine and had convinced him that we were not teaching the truth of God's Word. He had not only infected this young man; he had infected many other members of the church.

ANGRY AND SEPARATED

Before long, my Youth President became angry and separated himself from the church, and others followed. By then, it was obvious what was happening, and I decided to jump on this thing and stop it before it was too late. In the process, we lost six or eight of our best young people, but thank God it was not even more than that. Because of that wolf coming in, that wonderful young man, who had been so committed to the Lord and his church, remains confused to this day. You can't be too careful about these things.

In time, a whole cross section of people in the church were affected, until eventually that spirit did come to naught. But it was not an easy fight. When we could finally overcome it, we had to go to our knees and seek God about why this thing had happened in the first place, why we had not been more alert to detect it before it did so much damage.

In this hour, more than ever, we need to have our spiritual eyes opened to understand what is happening around us, and we must respect the power of covenant. When you make a covenant with someone, you can't break it, so don't make it in the first place unless you know what you're doing.

"WHO ARE YE?"

The story continues:

> And the men of Israel said unto the Hivites, Peradventure ye dwell among us; and how shall we make a league with you? And they said unto Joshua, We are thy servants. And Joshua said unto them, Who are ye? and from whence come ye? And they said unto him, From a very far country thy servants are come because of the name of the LORD thy God: for we have heard the fame of him, and all that he did in Egypt, And all that he did to the two kings of the Amorites,

that were beyond Jordan, to Sihon king of Heshbon, and to Og king of Bashan, which was at Ashtaroth.

Joshua 9:7-10

That all sounded wonderful. It was, in fact, just what the children of Israel wanted to hear. Of course, the enemy knew this all too well. This teaches us a very important lesson. We can't always go by what people say. We have to verify for ourselves if what they're saying is true. People often know what you want to hear, so that's what they say, whether it's the truth or not. Later, they may say something very different. We must be keen in the Spirit to see behind the words people speak.

Don't be so quick to believe everything you hear and to connect with everyone you meet. There are good connections and bad connections, and if we're too eager to connect, we will often make the bad type of connection.

EVEN JOSHUA WAS FOOLED

In the case of Israel, even Joshua was fooled. He was their leader, and he should have known what to do in this situation, but apparently he didn't. What his neighbors were saying was crafty and well-thought-out. The elders among them had planned it all very carefully and had given the men they sent careful instructions:

Wherefore our elders and all the inhabitants of our country spake to us, saying, Take victuals with you for the journey, and go to meet them, and say unto them,

We are your servants: therefore now make ye a league
with us. This our bread we took hot for our provision
out of our houses on the day we came forth to go unto
you; but now, behold, it is dry, and it is mouldy: and
these bottles of wine, which we filled, were new; and,
behold, they be rent: and these our garments and our
shoes are become old by reason of the very long jour-
ney.   Joshua 9:11-13

What cunning liars these were, and there are a lot
of talented liars alive in our generation as well. If you
haven't met them already, you will soon enough.

These particular men seemed to have physical proof
that what they were saying was true. So how can we
blame Joshua and his men for believing them? Can anyone detect that kind of lie unless they do it in the Spirit?

As these men told the lie of their long and arduous
journey, what they showed made it sound real, and believe me, in the days to come, you will be faced with
similar situations. If you are unable to detect a crafty lie,
you, too, will be fooled. We desperately need God to help
us know the real from the false, lest we be swept away by
crafty falsehoods.

SUBTLE LIES DECEIVE

The subtle lies spoken by these men, who supposedly
had come from afar, totally fooled Joshua and the elders
of Israel:

*And the men took of their victuals, and asked not
counsel at the mouth of the LORD. And Joshua made
peace with them, and made a league [covenant] with
them, to let them live: and the princes of the congregation sware unto them.*   Jeremiah 9:14-15

The "wise men" of Israel were fooled that day because
they could only see with their eyes and not with the
Spirit. They *"asked not counsel at the mouth of the LORD,"*
and that is always a deadly mistake.

To me this is one of the saddest passages of scripture
in the entire Bible. These men walked away from that
meeting thinking they had made a wise decision and
done a good deed. They were satisfied that what they had
done was for the benefit of everyone, and so there was a
bounce in their step, a joy in their spirits. But they could
not have been more wrong.

Now tell me, what would you have done in that situation? Knowing the circumstances and the subtleness of
the enemy's approach, would you have been able to detect the lies? Think about it.

SATAN'S LIES ARE UNCOVERED

It doesn't take long for Satan's lies to be uncovered. In
this case, just three days:

*And it came to pass at the end of three days after they
had made a league [covenant] with them, that they*

heard that they were their neighbours, and that they
dwelt among them.   Joshua 9:16

This was a problem because God had purposely given
Joshua and his people instructions to destroy their pagan
neighbors. This was to be His demonstration of wrath
upon unbelievers, mockers and scorners. Instead, Joshua
had been fooled into making a peace pact with them, and
now he could not go back on his word. This, then, caused
him to disobey God.

THIS HAD TO BE INVESTIGATED

When this news surfaced, the leaders of Israel went
out to see if it was true, and what they found caused great
consternation and great dissension among them. What
should they do now?

And the children of Israel journeyed, and came
unto their cities on the third day. Now their cities
were Gibeon, and Chephirah, and Beeroth, and Kir-
jathjearim. And the children of Israel smote them not,
because the princes of the congregation had sworn
unto them by the Lord God of Israel. And all the con-
gregation murmured against the princes. But all the
princes said unto all the congregation, We have sworn
unto them by the Lord God of Israel: now therefore
we may not touch them. This we will do to them; we
will even let them live, lest wrath be upon us, because
of the oath which we sware unto them.

And the princes said unto them, Let them live; but let them be hewers of wood and drawers of water unto all the congregation; as the princes had promised them.

Joshua 9:17-21

What a hard lesson this was! You cannot enter into a covenant lightly with anyone, no matter what things look like. The men of Israel had made their covenant, and so now they could not rescind it. They were a covenant-keeping people because they had a covenant-keeping God. When they gave their word, that was it. In this case, their misguided covenant led to tragedy.

JOSHUA'S CURSE

The result of this covenant was a curse. Joshua ended up with a hostile nation on his flanks because he failed to seek God about the covenant he made with the Gibeonites. As we noted, Israel suffered for years to come because of this decision. Eventually the Gibeonites, with their mocking and scorning ways, not only lived in nearby cities; they lived in the same city and the same house with Joshua, and yet he could not touch them. His vow prevented it.

Don't enter into a covenant with any person lightly, whether it be for business, marriage, or any other purpose. This is a serious matter. A covenant is sacred, binding and to be respected. Seek God before you make such a commitment.

Joshua, as great a man as he was, and his people, many of them considered princes and elders, were duped because they failed to do what was essential in such a situation: consult with the Creator and Ruler of the Universe.

PRAY ABOUT ABSOLUTELY EVERYTHING

We cannot emphasize too much: Pray about absolutely everything. If you will look back and examine the times when trouble came upon you, I believe you will see that often, if not always, it was because you did not consult God enough on the subject.

Should you pray about buying a car? Absolutely. You don't know what you're getting or where it's been, who had it, or how they treated it. You'd better pray, or you'll end up with a lemon, and it will cost you plenty.

If a car is too old, there may not be parts available for it. That's why someone else didn't buy it. The salesman tells you it's worth several thousand dollars, when he should have said it was worth only a fraction of that, and he'll be happy for you to take it off of his hands.

Should you pray about buying a house? Absolutely. Is that the part of town where God wants you to be? Is a certain house selling cheap because it's been eaten up with termites? Ask God first.

People say to me, "Pastor, when I saw the house I knew it was the right one because it was exactly the color the Lord told me to look for." Well, there's a lot more to a house than the color. Pray about it.

YOU CANNOT BE LED BY YOUR MIND

In making a covenant with someone, you cannot be led by your mind, no matter how intelligent you may be. No one has all the information available. Only God knows everything, so you must lean on Him. Imagine, Joshua was an intelligent man and a great leader, but he and the best of his advisors were fooled, and they made a terrible mistake. Pray about your situation.

Most Christians start out well, seeking God about everything. But, then, as they gain more self-confidence, they stop taking every little thing to God. And when you don't pray about a matter, you are going into it blindly. You need to know God's opinion on the matter.

If you are in school, before you sit down to write an exam, pray. Consult the Lord. Regardless of how well or how badly you think you're doing in a particular class, pray. You can't do anything without God.

SOMETHING NEW BEGINS TO HAPPEN

Through salvation, God opens our eyes that we might see, and His promise for the New Testament time is that, first of all, we will all know Him. Then, secondly, He promises that He will write His laws on our minds and on our hearts. When this is true, something else begins to happen. After you have known the Lord for a few months, you will begin to feel it when a thing is not right. If it doesn't seem right to you, that's God way of showing you that something is wrong with it. Heed these inner feelings and avoid the thing at all costs.

No one should have to take you by the hand and show you why a thing is right or not. You have the Knower inside of you, and He can guide you by letting you feel peace about a situation or not feel peace about it.

The promise of God's Word is this:

Howbeit when he, the Spirit of truth, is come, he will guide you into all truth.   John 16:13

We, then, have a great advantage over the days of Joshua. He did not have access to the Holy Ghost in the same way we do, to lead and guide us, and when we come up against a situation, we can feel in our inner man what the will of the Lord is and act accordingly.

DON'T IGNORE
YOUR SPIRITUAL SENSES

You don't have to understand all the reasons why, but if a thing doesn't seem good to you, just say, "I can't do that." Period! That settles it. It's not right for you.

When something doesn't feel right, but you keep trying to make it work, how can that be correct? You're just flirting with disaster. Eventually that thing will backfire, and you'll get hurt.

Flirting with disaster is what caused the explosion on that oil rig in the Gulf of Mexico in 2010 and brought about the greatest natural disaster in our nation's history and untold misery for our beloved Louisianans. Workmen on that rig were already complaining of feeling sick, but the drilling continued. All that was guiding the men behind that project was the greed of having millions of dollars in profits from their relatively meager investment. Warning signs were appearing on the computer systems, but they ignored them. Money is not a proper motivation, and following it will often lead to a sorrowful ending.

There are times in all of our lives when we need to heed the warning signals around us and shut down everything until we can understand what we're doing wrong and what different course we need to take. Seek God, and He will show you what to do. If you sincerely pray, God will answer. Don't wait until disaster strikes before you start praying.

PEOPLE LIKE THE STRANGE CABO

We have a bird in Trinidad called the cabo. This bird only works on building a house when rain comes. If the rain ends before the house is finished, he stops the construction. Every time it rains you will see him with a twig in his mouth, hard at work, and every time the rain stops, you will see him going on his merry way, doing his own thing. This reminds me of so many foolish people. They only get serious when their life or livelihood is threatened, and only pray when they are in trouble.

Most people pray when a State trooper is approaching their car, because they have been caught speeding and are about to pay the price. "Please help me, Lord," they plead. But isn't it a little late for that? Smokey is on their tail because the sign said 60 MPH, and they were caught going more than 80. If you love life, don't take so many chances with it. The Scriptures admonish us:

> *See then that ye walk circumspectly, not as fools, but as wise, redeeming the time, because the days are evil. Wherefore be ye not unwise, but understanding what the will of the Lord is.* Ephesians 5:15-17

This message can help you to stop making the kinds of foolish mistakes you've made in the past. There are certain things that you must leave alone, others that you need to forget entirely and then learn to wait on the Lord.

LEARN TO WAIT ON GOD

We spoke of waiting on God in situations of personal attraction, dating and marriage, but the truth is that it is vital in absolutely everything. Again, God has promised:

> *But they that wait upon the LORD shall renew their strength; they shall mount up with wings as eagles; they shall run, and not be weary; and they shall walk, and not faint.* Isaiah 40:31

We usually start out waiting on God, but then we feel that we have waited too long already, and we take matters into our own hands. That's when we get ourselves into trouble. People who do their own thing must suffer the consequences.

Personally, I feel that time is too short to make many mistakes, and I have not served God all these years to lose out now. I refuse to be wasted by the devil. How sad it would be to walk with the King for so many years and then let the devil sidetrack me. No matter what comes my way, I intend to keep my eyes on Jesus.

AVOIDING FOOLISH MISTAKES

Why is it that so many preachers wait until they are older before they "mess up"? They walk with God all though their youth, and are faithful, and then they make a foolish mistake that sidelines them before their time. Suddenly, at sixty or sixty-five, they are wearing fancy boots and the latest style Italian shoes and wanting everyone to notice them. Those days should be long gone.

Personally, I intend to hold on to God because I know that He is faithful. I have committed everything to Him, and I know that He is able to keep it until the end. I am determined not to become a reproach to His Kingdom, and I seek Him every single day to keep me strong in His Spirit. I want to be a testimony, not only to the world around me, but also to the entire Christian community.

If you are at the point of making some serious decisions about life, ask God to give you the necessary tools to decide well.

OUR GREATEST ALLEGIANCE IS TO GOD

Never make a covenant with anyone without first seeking the will of God. Our greatest allegiance is always to Him. When we have made a commitment to Him and His Church, we cannot afford to make worldly alliances and ungodly commitments, and we cannot afford to make foolish promises. Know who God wants you to be in covenant with, and don't take anyone else's word for it. Get on your knees before Him and wait until you hear His voice in the matter.

Because God created the concept of covenant, He alone knows best when it comes to these things. Don't do anything at all without consulting Him, and since a covenant is so important, whatever you do don't enter into any covenant without guidance from Him. Begin today *Discovering the Untapped Power of Covenant.*

Chapter 22

COVENANTS THAT SHOULD BE BROKEN

And Jephthah vowed a vow unto the Lord, and said, If thou shalt without fail deliver the children of Ammon into mine hands, then it shall be, that whatsoever cometh forth of the doors of my house to meet me, when I return in peace from the children of Ammon, shall surely be the Lord's, and I will offer it up for a burnt offering. So Jephthah passed over unto the children of Ammon to fight against them; and the Lord delivered them into his hands. Judges 11:30-32

There are covenants that should be broken, and one such example is found in the sad and amazing story of Jephthah, one of the judges who governed Israel before the rise of the kings. He made a rash vow to God, and the outcome was not at all what he had intended.

JEPHTHAH'S RASH VOW

Jephthah vowed to God that if He would give him victory in battle against his enemies, he would sacrifice the first thing that came through the door of his house upon his return. He must have imagined that it would be a sheep or some other animal, but to his utter dismay, when he returned home victorious from battle, his only child, a beautiful daughter, came out to meet him, dancing, singing and rejoicing to celebrate her father's victory. The story ends very sadly with Jephthah actually carrying out his vow and sacrificing his precious daughter.

To my way of thinking, this was a foolish covenant and one that should have been broken. Personally, I would have not have made it in the first place, and if I had mistakenly done it, I would have broken it. There are things that will put you in trouble, and if that is the case, leave them alone.

ISN'T THAT CONTRADICTORY?

"But," you might protest, "isn't that contradictory? You've been saying throughout the book that covenants must be kept." Yes, that's true, but if keeping some promise you've made, either to God or man, will send you to Hell, then forget about it. It's not worth it, and it's not the right thing for you to do. God won't hold you to a promise that was made foolishly.

Personally I don't have much respect for Jephthah, considering him to have been an ignorant and foolish man. I wouldn't kill a child for any covenant. In one way I can understand where he was coming from. He had expected a cow or some other animal and not his child, and he did keep his word. But God does not expect us to do what is not right, covenant or no covenant.

There are some covenants that should not be kept. Obviously, you need to seek God in this matter and let Him guide you. But don't ever fall into this trap of doing something illegal or immoral because of a promise.

Just because you *can* make a mistake, don't be afraid to covenant. Instead, start today *Discovering the Untapped Power of Covenant.*

Part VI

WHAT ALL BELIEVERS NEED TO DO

Chapter 23

THIS IS A COVENANT WORTH REJOICING OVER

Rejoice in the Lord always: and again I say, Rejoice.
Philippians 4:4

This is a covenant worth rejoicing over, and anyone who does not rejoice in it has not yet understood it.

LEARN FROM THE WORLD

We have much to learn from the world in this regard. In 1989 the Atlanta Braves won the World Series, and the rejoicing from the stadium in Atlanta could be heard forty miles away. We, too, have something to be excited about and when you get excited, people know about it.

When our New Orleans Saints won the Super Bowl in February of 2010 (after many years of lackluster play), the people of Louisiana got excited and put some of us church folk to shame. The Saints won the Super Bowl just that once and did not repeat the next year, but we have something to be excited about every single day of our lives. God has made us some wonderful promises, and He always keeps His Word.

GET EXCITED

If you're not excited about God and His loving favor toward you, why would anyone else want to hear your testimony or have you pray for them? Abram was excited enough about God to leave his country and his kindred and make a long and uncertain journey. He could do that because he had a promise from God, and you have great promises too.

We are the real saints, and so, Saints of God, it's time to rejoice. On any given day, you may not feel your best. You may not be on top of the world, but let the Spirit of God place within you a praise that will overcome every circumstance of your life.

Press through! It's time to sing praises, time to clap your hands and stomp your feet. It's time to say, "I love You, Lord," time to rejoice in the benefits of our wonderful covenant.

Do it today and start *Discovering the Untapped Power of Covenant.*

Chapter 24

THIS IS A COVENANT WORTH PURSUING

Wherefore do ye spend money for that which is not bread? and your labour for that which satisfieth not? hearken diligently unto me, and eat ye that which is good, and let your soul delight itself in fatness.

Isaiah 55:2

For too long, we have wasted our resources on that which is not eternal, so now we must take stock. These are hard times, and we are all being more careful about how we spend our money. In a spiritual sense, why spend on that which quickly passes and fails to satisfy? This is not real *"bread."*

SEEK SOMETHING REAL FOR A CHANGE

For our life's work to become meaningful and our daily expenditures to bear eternal fruit, we need to pursue

God and His ways, real "bread." It's time to do what God demands, hearkening unto Him and eating what is truly *"good."* Instead of wasting your time and energy on passing things, pursue something that will bring you ultimate benefit. Pursue God's covenant promises.

In the natural sense, all of us like to eat things that are not good for us. Our taste buds tell us that this is what we want, but, at the same time, our good sense tells us that it will not be good for us in the long run, and therefore we should leave it alone. What you like to eat and what you need for good health are often two very different things.

GOOD TASTE VS. GOOD HEALTH

For instance: Oh, how we love our fried foods! But when we give in and eat them, we suffer the consequences. After forty especially our eating habits have to change. There are certain meats that we cannot continue to eat. That's just the reality. Those who don't believe it are doomed to suffer the consequences.

If God said, *"Eat that which is good,"* then it behooves each of us to maintain a health consciousness (both in the natural and in the spiritual). If you hope to live a long life and do it without pain *"and let your soul delight itself in fatness,"* then you need to obey God's Word and *"eat that which is good."* Why would He say it if He didn't mean it? And would He even say it if it was not important?

GOD WILL WORK FOR YOU IF YOU WILL PURSUE WHAT'S WORTHWHILE

God's Word continues:

Incline your ear, and come unto me: hear, and your soul shall live; and I will make an everlasting covenant with you, even the sure mercies of David. Behold, I have given him for a witness to the people, a leader and commander to the people. Isaiah 55:2-3

God is ready to do this same work for you. Are you ready to abandon the pursuit of things that don't satisfy and pursue His will for your life instead? It must be a joint effort. Each must do his part.

JOY AWAITS YOU

God said:

To appoint unto them that mourn in Zion, to give unto them beauty for ashes, the oil of joy for mourning, the garment of praise for the spirit of heaviness; that they might be called trees of righteousness, the planting of the LORD, that he might be glorified. Isaiah 61:3

This is a word for today, for this is exactly what God wants to do among us. Zion is the Church of today, and God is not pleased that we mourn and that we sit in ashes. His will is to *appoint* us and to give us beauty for

199

ashes. If you are among those who mourn, God wants to give you *"the oil of joy."* If you are among those who have a *"spirit of heaviness,"* He wants to give you *"a garment of praise."* Whenever you feel that spirit of heaviness upon you, it's time to shake yourself and start praising God.

This will bring you back to the place you should rightly be in God, so that you can be called a tree *"of righteousness, the planting of the LORD, that he might be glorified."*

God went on to declare:

And they shall build the old wastes, they shall raise up the former desolations, and they shall repair the waste cities, the desolations of many generations.

Isaiah 61:4

It's time for some rebuilding and some restoration in your life. Don't put it off. Start today. The stakes are very high.

MEN SHALL CALL YOU ...

What else will happen?

And strangers shall stand and feed your flocks, and the sons of the alien shall be your plowmen and your vinedressers. But ye shall be named the Priests of the LORD: men shall call you the Ministers of our God: ye shall eat the riches of the Gentiles, and in their glory shall ye boast yourselves.　　Isaiah 61:5-6

In ourselves, we have nothing to boast about, but we can surely boast in the Lord and in His goodness to us. I am not in this world by man's assignment; rather I'm here on assignment from the living God. And when God lifts you up, no devil can put you down. When God blesses you, the devil can't curse you. Men will sing your praises when you get serious about the things of God and start pursuing that which never fades or rots and cannot be stolen.

SHAKE OFF MEN'S CURSES

Refuse to accept any negative word from others. Don't accept men's curses upon your life. Believe what God has said, that you will live victoriously and supernaturally in this world, come what may.

You were destined to tell the nations that Jesus Christ is Lord. It doesn't matter how bad things look. It doesn't matter what uncaring people told you when you were young. Someone may have said, "You can't make it," but that's not God's determination.

Some contend that evil words spoken over us in our youth have no effect, but they're wrong. Such words have a deep and devastating effect. When negative words are spoken over you by someone in authority, it can be devastating. To overcome these things, you must immerse yourself in the Word of God (His covenant promises for you). Say to yourself what God has said about you:

No weapon that is formed against thee shall prosper;
and every tongue that shall rise against thee in judg-

201

ment thou shalt condemn. This is the heritage of the servants of the LORD, and their righteousness is of me, saith the LORD.   Isaiah 54:17

Say it until it becomes personal and you know you can claim it for yourself. Then you will have complete deliverance and complete victory over all those negative influences. Until then, your life may seem to be going around in circles, going nowhere. God wants to bring you out from that situation and allow you to partake of the benefits of the wonderful covenant He offers you today.

YOU ARE WHAT GOD SAYS YOU ARE

What is God's will for you:

But ye shall be named the Priests of the LORD: men shall call you the Ministers of our God: ye shall eat the riches of the Gentiles, and in their glory shall ye boast yourselves.   Isaiah 61:6

Don't let men call you anything but what God says you are. Insist on being what the Word of God has declare for you. You can be what the Word of God says you are, you can do what the Word of God says you can do, and you can say what the Word of God says you can say.

Stop living your life to please others. Stop patterning your life after people around you. Rebuke the spirits that would have you conform to the ideals of others. Instead, rise up to declare these scriptural truths:

THIS IS A COVENANT WORTH PURSUING

I can do all things through Christ which strengtheneth me. Philippians 4:13

Greater is he that is in [me] than he that is in the world. 1 John 4:4

Those who would forced you to conform to their will have nothing to offer you. They have no Heaven for you to dwell in, no eternal life for you to enjoy. There is only One who has the power to consign us to Heaven (or to Hell if we fail to heed His call), so let us serve Him. Let us receive His Word. Let us live by His everlasting covenant. This is a covenant worth pursuing.

BOAST OF HIS GOODNESS

In the days ahead, as you contemplate the benefits of your covenant with God, become bold for the Lord and begin to boast of His goodness in your life. If you don't do it, who will? If you don't get happy about what He has done for you, who will? If you don't let His love lift you up out of the place you're in, who will do it for you? If you won't rejoice, who will do it for you?

Refuse to have a pity party. Refuse to walk around with your head down, feeling like everything is over. Know that help is on the way even now. You may experience a down day, but you're not alone by any stretch of the imagination. God is your help—on good days and on bad. So don't give up.

Doubts may dim your sky, but God has promised to answer you by and by. Good things will surely come to those who wait upon the Lord, so wait patiently and expectantly upon Him. If you are pursuing His ways, you can't lose.

"THE MINISTERS OF GOD"

But ye shall be named the Priests of the LORD: men shall call you the Ministers of our God: ye shall eat the riches of the Gentiles, and in their glory shall ye boast yourselves. Isaiah 61:6

You are *"the Ministers of our God."* Wow! This word doesn't just refer to those who stand behind a sacred desk. If you have received something from God, you can then minister what you have to others.

Each of us may have a little different ministry, but each of us has one, for we are all vital parts of the Body of Christ.

YOU SHALL HAVE DOUBLE

Isaiah didn't stop there. He said:

For your shame ye shall have double; and for confusion they shall rejoice in their portion: therefore in their land they shall possess the double: everlasting joy shall be unto them. For I the LORD love judgment, I hate robbery for burnt offering; and I will direct their work in truth, and I will make an everlasting covenant with them.   Isaiah 61:7-8

Who is the *"them"* referred to in this verse? It is all those who will choose to follow the Lord in covenant relationship, and that includes you and me. We're part of the New Covenant, and we also have a personal covenant with God. Don't let the devil tell you any differently, and don't accept anything less.

Determine today that you will live for the Lord all the days of your life. Then don't let your resolves dim after only a day or two. With the help of the Lord, let your relationship with God be what you (and He) have determined it to be, an everlasting covenant.

LET YOUR LIFE BE A CHALLENGE TO OTHERS

Because of what God has done in my life, many other ministers from Trinidad have been challenged, and that's what God wants to do for you too. When people see your lifestyle lived out before them, it should provoke them to jealousy and cause them to want to have what you have. If you don't get excited about it, who else will?

"THEIR SEED SHALL BE KNOWN"

And their seed shall be known among the Gentiles, and their offspring among the people: all that see them shall acknowledge them, that they are the seed which the LORD *hath blessed.*   Isaiah 61:9

You may not have physical seed, offspring from your own body, but you can have spiritual seed that is *"known among the Gentiles."* God will do it for you.

IGNORE THE DOOMSAYERS

Our God is a covenant-keeping God and He promises that just as long as the sun continues to rule over the day and the moon over the night, His relationship with His people will continue. Don't be shaken by the doom-sayers of our time. Way back before 1988, a man wrote a very persuasive book entitled *88 Reasons Why Jesus Will Come in 1988*, and he had people running around terrified. But the world did not come to an end in 1988.

Then, again, when we were nearing the beginning of this new millennium, many predicted catastrophe and doom upon the whole world. Life as we knew it, they said, would soon end. Again, it did not happen.

In 2011, as this book was in preparation, a similar prediction was made, but nothing came of it. We should expect more dates to be cited in the near future as the end of the world, but the truth is that no man knows the day nor the hour. Jesus Himself said it:

But of that day and hour knoweth no man, no, not the angels of heaven, but my Father only.

Matthew 24:36

Not even the angels know. Only God knows the day when He will send Jesus back to Earth. In the meantime, we will pass through many troubles and problems, but God knows how to protect His own.

What is important is that you and I busy ourselves pursuing the covenant promises of God so that, whenever that day comes, we will have no regrets but will have eternal treasures to lay at the feet of our Savior.

Why not give it a try? Begin today *Discovering the Untapped Power of Covenant.*

Chapter 25

THIS IS A COVENANT WORTH COMMITTING YOURSELF TO

For I know whom I have believed, and am persuaded that he is able to keep that which I have committed unto him against that day.　　2 Timothy 1:12

This is a covenant worth committing yourself to. The thing that you commit to Christ He will keep. If you commit your whole life to Him, He will keep it. Commit your thoughts to Him, and He will keep them. If you commit nothing to Him, then He cannot keep anything for you.

YOU ONLY GET OUT WHAT YOU PUT IN

Your bank can only credit to your account as much money as you entrust to it. The officials of the bank cannot allow you to withdraw more than you have deposited. What you put into it is exactly what you can get out of it.

It's the same with God. If you invest time in prayer, you will get something in return. If nothing else, you will be strengthened. If you're not happy with your life and you want God to make a change for you, then you have to meet Him halfway. You have to make certain sacrifices if you expect Him to work for you. Remember, this covenant is a mutually binding agreement, and God will do His part, but you must also do yours.

An example of something many need to do to get rid of in order to reap the benefits of covenant is this: you cannot fill your mind and heart with pornography and expect God to bless you. You need to get such things out of your system first. As a child of God, there are other things that we cannot do. If you want to know Him and enjoy the benefits of His covenant life, then you have to make some changes in yours.

HE CAN KEEP IT ALL

Our God is able to keep all that I commit to Him, but what do I need to commit to Him? The answer is: Absolutely everything!

Even commit your failures to Him. Some would rather not mention them, but we must face the fact that we fail and commit those failures to His goodness. He can handle them and help us not to repeat them.

When you go to a doctor, you tell him as much as you can about your condition so that he can make a proper diagnosis of your problem. Why would you trust the Lord any less?

Try this: Go to your doctor, and when he asks what is ailing you, say, "Well, I'd rather not talk about it. It's embarrassing to me. I just want to forget it and hope that others forget it too."

Or try just saying, "Oh, nothing in particular."

When he asks, "Then why are you here?" you can answer, "Oh, just for a visit."

When he asks, "Well, what do you want me to do?" tell him "Just give me a check-up."

He'll say, "Okay, but what am I checking for specifically?"

HE NEEDS AN ANSWER FROM YOU

Your doctor needs an answer from you, for your kind of approach clearly won't work. So, why, when we go to God, do some say, "Well, God, You know everything," and they fail to submit their worst failures to Him? If we could hear God's voice today, He might be saying, "What do you really want from Me? What exactly do you want Me to do for you?"

Most of us might answer, "Well, Lord, I want to commit everything to You."

"But what specifically are you committing to Me?" He might ask.

"You know everything, God," we might answer.

Yes, He knows everything. You're not wrong about that. But He wants to hear you committing each thing specifically to His care, trusting His love for you, even when you fail, and trusting His power to keep you from failing again.

211

Most of us are quick to commit all of our good points to God, and that's fine, but what about the bad? That's a part of us also, and it needs to be committed to the care of a loving and caring heavenly Father.

THINGS WE FEEL BAD ABOUT

There are things that we feel bad about. We experience downfalls. Not everything is a victory for us. We have our downs as well as our ups, and God can help us with all of these things, but we too often prefer to maintain all of this as some sort of secret.

How foolish! God knows the secrets of every heart.

> *Shall not God search this out? for he knoweth the secrets of the heart.* Psalm 44:21

We cannot hide anything from God. So, yes, He already knows about it, but He wants you to voluntarily commit it to Him in faith that He will not despise you for your failings and that He can help you overcome them (if you will only acknowledge your need of His help in this area).

HE CAN CHANGE IT

The moment you commit a situation to God, He can change it. Why, then, would you go through life carrying that heavy baggage alone, not letting Him deal with it? You're like a Christian Atlas, trying to carry the burden of the whole world on your shoulders.

A COVENANT WORTH COMMITTING YOURSELF TO

We men are fortunate in that we don't carry purses. I don't know how women can carry so much around all the time. But we do carry heavy burdens in our hearts. We have much that needs to get out so that we can be freed from it. Let God do some housecleaning in your heart today. Commit everything to Him.

WHAT'S BEHIND THE DOOR?

When we visit people's homes, it is always quickly evident how good a housekeeper they are (or aren't, as the case may be). What if we looked behind the refrigerator? What would we find? What if we looked under the rug? What would that look like? Has something been swept under there and left?

What am I trying to say? Expose everything to God and let Him deal with it. Stop trying to hide the dirt in your life. You can't hide it from Him anyway, and you're only fooling yourself. If you commit it all to Him, then He can deal with it once and for all.

Why would we purposely expose ourselves to God in this way? Because we want Him to bless us and take us to a new level. We must come face to face with the living, covenant-keeping God and walk with Him, and anything that hinders us in this pursuit must be committed to Him, so He can deal with it.

GOD DIDN'T NEED OUR HELP

God didn't tell us we had to understand how to make a covenant with Him. He did all that for us. He has made the covenant. All we have to do is commit to it and walk in it. He has opened a way for us. We just need to take advantage of that way.

God didn't ask us to help Him create the world. If He had left it up to us where to locate the Euphrates River and which way it should run, we would have made a mess of it. He created this whole world for us to enjoy and then left us to decide how we will walk in it.

God didn't need your help to know how to form the Jordan Valley. He knew how to do that. And He also knew how to make the most wonderful covenant ever conceived.

CHECK OUT HIS PROMISES

You'd better check out the Book of His covenant promises. It is holy and true.

It can take you weeks to get through one portion of it, but if you stick with it, you'll make it. Stick like a stamp on a letter until it reaches its final destination. If the stamp comes off halfway through the process, the letter will be returned to the sender.

I don't know about you, but I'm determined not to go back. I'm determined that God will take me through as I continue to commit my life to Him.

There are areas of my life in which I have to ask God to be patient with me while I get my act together, and I boldly ask the Holy Ghost to help me know how to have victory in those areas. But one thing I do: I never look back, thinking it might be better to return to where I came from. Never! With all of our struggles, we must keep moving forward.

Why not start today and begin *Discovering the Untapped Power of Covenant?*

Chapter 26

BREAKING THIS COVENANT HAS CONSEQUENCES

Now Israel went out against the Philistines to battle.

1 Samuel 4:1

Normally, when the people of Israel went out to battle against their enemies, their victory was assured, but this time something was different. In the first round of fighting, the Philistines prevailed and killed some four thousand Israeli soldiers.

STUNNED

When this happened, the elders of the people were stunned and questioned among themselves why this evil thing had happened. They decided to send for the Ark of the Covenant, a piece of holy furniture created for the Wilderness Tabernacle in the time of Moses and the Exodus, that housed the tables of stone upon which were written the Ten Commandments, a pot containing some of the manna God had miraculously provided for them in their wilderness journey and Aaron's rod that had budded, revealing God's choice for the holy priesthood. In the wilderness Tabernacle, this ark had represented the place of God's dwelling, and they needed Him now as never before.

THE ARK WAS A REMINDER OF THEIR AGREEMENT WITH GOD

The Ark of the Covenant was a reminder, in this moment of stunned defeat and mind-numbing loss, of the agreement God had made with His people on Mt. Sinai so many years before. He had given them specific instructions about how to make that Ark, of what to make it and who was to make it. It was to be special, and it was to be portable so that they could carry it with them wherever they went.

But the people of Israel had to come to terms with the fact that the current generation didn't understand just who God was and what it meant to have a covenant with Him. This is something that every new generation must discover for itself. He is a covenant-keeping God, but each generation must renew the covenant. That box reminded them of this fact.

A VERY SPECIAL BOX

It was a very elegant box, covered with beaten gold, and on the top of it were the wings of cherubims. But it was what was inside that made the Ark of the Covenant truly unique. Those thee items revealed God's faithfulness in covenant with His people and, therefore, they were the most sacred possessions of the nation. The Ark was sent for now and brought to the front, in the hope that it would encourage the people and bring them the blessed victory they needed.

This should teach us all a valuable lesson. When you find yourself in trouble of any kind, remember the covenant you have made with God and get His presence on the scene to help you. With God fighting for you, you cannot lose.

God has made many promises to you, but you have also made many promises to Him. You have said you would live for Him and His glory, serve Him in any way He desired and would tell everyone about His goodness. Have you kept your covenant with God? No? Is that perhaps the root of the problems you are currently going through? If so, recognize it, welcome God's presence with you again, and He will step onto the scene and take over the battle for you. The enemy thought he had you and was about to devour you, but God can turn things around in a flash.

Is your back against the wall? Does there seem to be no way of escape for you? Does calamity seem imminent? Turn to your ever-faithful covenant-keeping God, and He will step in and turn the situation to your favor. In the midst of your calamity, your distress, and your persecution, God will fight your battles and bring you the victory. Jesus can be a fence around you.

JESUS, BE A FENCE AROUND ME

Fred Hammond sings an age-old song with these powerful words:

Jesus, be a fence all around me everyday.
Jesus, I want You to protect me as I travel along the way.
I know You can
I know You will
Fight my battle
If I just keep still.
Lord, be a fence all around me everyday.

Is He your protection today?

THE ARK WAS BROUGHT

Now things got more interesting for the children of Israel. The Ark of the Covenant was brought from Shiloh, accompanied by the two sons of Eli, the priest. When it arrived in the camp, the people were so relieved and overjoyed that they sent up a great shout that shook the earth beneath them. Hearing this shout, the Philistines became alarmed, and rightly so. They knew enough about these people to know what their Ark symbolized, and they knew they were in trouble. All the pagan neighbors of Israel knew of the strength of their God and His special agreement with His people. They knew and trembled.

This has not changed in our age of enlightenment. The God we serve is strong, and if we are willing to covenant with Him and we keep our part of the bargain, He will always stand with us in our hour of need. In your darkest hour, He will be there. Count on it.

THE PHILISTINES FEARED

The Philistines had heard many stories of God's rescue of His people, and so now they were afraid. Hear their words:

> *Woe unto us! who shall deliver us out of the hand of these mighty Gods? these are the Gods that smote the Egyptians with all the plagues in the wilderness.*
> 1 Samuel 4:8

Their theology wasn't very good, but they knew enough about God to be afraid. They had not been afraid of the backslidden armies of Israel, but they were afraid of this *"mighty"* God who now stood with those armies.

Today we understand that the ancient Ark of the Covenant was a mere shadow of the cross of Jesus to come and what it would do to give us total victory. The manifest presence of God was with that Ark, and Jesus, God

Himself, veiled in human flesh, was there dying on the cross. His blood that was shed that day had been foreshadowed in the offerings of the wilderness Tabernacle.

Although the Philistines were initially fearful that day (knowing the power of the God of covenant), the more they thought about it, the more they became convinced that they could defeat the Israelites. Their enemy had just not been up to par recently. They had slipped considerably in their resolve, and that's why the Philistines had dared to attack them in the first place. "Come on," someone said, "we can take these Israelites," and the battle was resumed.

THIS TIME,
THE PHILISTINES WERE RIGHT

Sadly, the Philistines were right this time. They not only prevailed in battle; the sacred Ark of the Covenant was captured, and the two sons of Eli, the priest, were killed.

A runner was sent to tell Eli what had happened. If the news that his two sons had died was not bad enough, the news that the Ark had been stolen was totally devastating to him.

Imagine it. All those years, Eli had given his life as a priest to maintain and protect the anointing of God over this people, and now, in a moment of weakness and backsliding, the people had allowed it to be stolen. The enemy had taken the most sacred things from Israel. To them, this was a tragedy of immense proportions.

GUARD AND PROTECT
THE ANOINTING

Do you understand how important it is to guard and protect the anointing in your life and in the lives of your loved ones? We must not allow material things to distract us from what is most important. The desires of our flesh must not be allowed to rob us of our future in God. Let's put it even more bluntly: Don't let a few moments of sexual pleasure take you out of God's favor and cause you to lose what is most valuable in life.

Stand strong to maintain and protect all that God has entrusted to your care. If you lose it, it could be for eternity. Five minutes of sexual enjoyment often lead to a lifetime of regret. Afterward, you weep with sorrow, but your tears cannot change what has happened.

ELI WAS DEVASTATED

When Eli received this message, that the sacred Ark had been lost in battle and that his two sons had also died, his heart melted in him, and he fell backward, broke his neck and died. Why did this terrible tragedy have to happen? Because covenant had been broken. God had never failed to keep His part, and this fact struck fear into the hearts of the Philistines, but the people of Israel had not kept their part, and this knowledge empowered their enemies to defeat them. Break the covenant, and you will suffer the consequences. Keep it, and you will live.

Start today *Discovering the Untapped Power of Covenant.*

Part VII

WHAT WILL YOUR DECISION BE?

Chapter 27

WHAT WILL YOU DO WITH THE COVENANT GOD OFFERS YOU TODAY?

Come unto me, all ye that labour and are heavy laden, and I will give you rest. Take my yoke upon you, and learn of me; for I am meek and lowly in heart: and ye shall find rest unto your souls. For my yoke is easy, and my burden is light. Matthew 11:28-30

God is speaking to you today in love and saying, "I will cleanse you from all unrighteousness." His hand is extended to you right now.

STILL ROOM FOR ONE

The songwriter Ira Stanphill said it well:

Tho millions have come,
There is still room for one.
Yes, there's room at the cross for you.

Jesus paid it all. Back there on Golgotha's hill, when His blood was spilled, He was making an entryway for you and for me. No longer do we have to look to the rudiments of this world and live in despair and unbelief or live in frustration because of our inability to keep a series of commandments. We have a hope for a better future here on Earth and an eternity with God Himself.

WE HAVE A BLESSED HOPE

Our hope is to one day look into the face of Jesus and receive what He paid for on Calvary. If you are sick, He can heal you. If you are down, He can lift you up. If you are weak, He can strengthen you. It was for this reason that the Bible says:

Let the weak say, I am strong.   Joel 3:10

You may be weak in yourself, but God promises:

I can do all things through Christ which strengtheneth me.   Philippians 4:13

Greater is he that is in you, than he that is in the world.   1 John 4:4

We have Heaven's backing. Sometimes it seems that we won't be able to make this journey. Sometimes the pressures of life come upon us, and we don't know where to turn or who to turn to, but if we keep looking to the

Lord, we will prevail. It's guaranteed in the covenant.

Sometimes we say, "God, when will it happen?" And He answers, "If you'll just hold on, it will surely come to pass."

I can't say for sure what you may be going through today, but what I can say is that God wants to cut a covenant with you. For those of you who know the Lord already, you've had these promises since the day you got saved, but maybe you're like many who have not really known what they had.

To many, it's all about joining a church and entering into fellowship with other believers. But the covenant we have entered into with God provides for so much more than that. We have given our lives to Him, and now you must say, "My life is not my own; to You I belong," and then let Him have His way with us.

GOD IS SPEAKING TO YOU TODAY

The Lord is saying to you today, as He did to ancient Israel:

> *I call heaven and earth to record this day against you, that I have set before you life and death, blessing and cursing: therefore choose life, that both thou and thy seed may live.*   Deuteronomy 30:19

Keeping covenant with God means life, and breaking it means death. What will your choice be? Of course, no one would willingly choose death. Right? But when we choose to reject a covenant with God or we choose to break covenant with God, we have chosen death by default.

HE IS A JEALOUS GOD

We love to speak of God and His love, but along with His love, we must also speak of God's jealousy over us. He is a loving God, and therefore He is also a jealous God. He loves us with an everlasting love, but He cannot stand the way His creatures treat Him and how they live.

Still, He offers us a way of escape. Jesus said: *"Come unto me, all ye that labour and are heavy laden, and I will give you rest. Take my yoke upon you, and learn of me; for I am meek and lowly in heart: and ye shall find rest unto your souls. For my yoke is easy, and my burden is light."*

ARE YOU "HEAVY LADEN" TODAY?

What does *"heavy laden"* mean? It means you are sorrowful, disgusted, feeling like you can't make it, that everybody's against you, just watching for you to make a mistake or fail. If that's you, Jesus is ready to make a new covenant with you today.

If you are a believer already, the New Testament promises:

> *If we confess our sins, he is faithful and just to forgive us our sins, and to cleanse us from all unrighteousness.* 1 John 1:9

This is all part of the New Covenant.

BEING SAVED

God's Word teaches:

For with the heart man believeth unto righteousness; and with the mouth confession is made unto salvation. Romans 10:10

The Scriptures have made it so easy, so simple, that anyone can understand it and obey:

For whosoever shall call upon the name of the Lord shall be saved. Romans 10:13

Has anyone been excluded from this invitation? *Whosoever* makes it complete and all-encompassing, doesn't it? Who would dare deny that you are included?

TO THE TEMPLE

In Old Testament times, you had to come to the Temple bearing an offering of a turtle dove or something much more substantial in order to be accepted by God. If you had sinned, everyone knew it because you had to walk down the street with your sacrificial animal, and the bigger the sin, the bigger the animal had to be. So when men and women stood on the street corner and saw you going by with a big ram, they knew what was up. There was no way for you to hide your wrongdoing. "Oh, my," people said. "Look what he did." It was even worse if you came with a big bull.

CITIES OF REFUGE

Eventually Israel had to establish cities of refuge for those who had committed involuntary manslaughter (murder without intent) and needed to escape the wrath of society. Yes, these were people of God, but wherever you have people, they're going to mess up from time to time because that's what people do.

In the Church, people mess up, just like they do in the world. The difference should be that we know what to do when we mess up.

When someone in Israel committed what we now call involuntary manslaughter, they ran to one of these cities, and there they were welcomed with open arms. If the person could remain in that city for seven years, he would then be forgiven and could be restored to his family.

Can you imagine being isolated in that way for seven years? How terrible! Now forgiveness is so simple, *"Come unto Me, and I will give you rest."*

HEAR THE INVITATION

If you are exhausted from going through the same situation over and over again, hear the invitation of Jesus: *"Come unto Me, and I will give you rest."*

Some people bring trouble upon themselves. They sin and repent and sin and repent until they become wearied by the cycle of their own failure. Jesus says to these, *"Come unto Me, and I will give you rest."*

Some people have failed so many times that they now expect it and aren't surprised when it comes. Jesus says to them today, *"Come unto Me, and I will give you rest."*

WHAT SHOULD YOU DO?

So what should you do? Just take a few minutes alone with God. Bow your spirit before Him and allow Him to work in you. His Spirit will reveal sin in you and areas that need change.

When you see a sin in your own life, it's okay to be sorrowful about it, but don't let it discourage you. Jesus wants to give you rest, not make you sad.

Don't try to change the thing yourself. We've all struggled with that and failed. Instead, let Him do the changing. You can't change yourself, but He can do it for you.

Right now, He is saying to you, *"Come unto Me, and I will give you rest."* And He will. Believe Him. Trust Him. Commit to Him. He offers you the best covenant ever conceived. Take it quickly and willingly, and you'll never be sorry.

YOU NEED TO KNOW THAT YOU'RE CHANGED

Today you need to know that you have been changed. You need to know that you've been born again. You need to make a covenant with God. You will live for Him, and, in return, He will do for you what you cannot do for yourself. Come to Him today, for He is waiting for you with open arms.

When you change, you can then change your whole family and your whole community. If you are saddened by the lifestyle being lived by people around you today and by the terrible waves of crime that are sweeping over our cities, know that God's desire is to make a great family, a great community and a great nation of you. He is saying to you today: I will make of YOU a great nation. So stop criticizing everyone else, and start changing your world.

GOD IS STILL IN CONTROL

God is still in control in this twenty-first century. He is still the Lord of the winds, waves and waters. He is still Lord of the mountains and Lord of all their resources. He is still Lord over every valley. Why not let Him have His way with you today?

Scientists may doubt that a certain thing is possible, but our God is Lord over the scientists and the science. There is not a man alive who can make rain fall from the sky. Try as they might, they always fail. God alone holds the key to the heavens.

One man said to me, "I don't believe in God."

"Can you make a green leaf?" I asked him.

"Of course not," he answered.

"You see," I said, "only God can do that."

That day all of his atheism went out the window, and he began to believe that God is God. Our God is mighty to save and strong to deliver.

WHAT DO YOU NEED TODAY?

What do you need from God today? Whatever it is, He has it.

This is your day for deliverance. Lay your petition before Him, and He will respond to it. Call upon Him, and He will hear and answer you. He has said:

> *Call unto me, and I will answer thee, and show thee great and mighty things, which thou knowest not.*
> Jeremiah 33:3

Why not give Him a try? What do you have to lose? He is just waiting to go to work on your behalf.

My friend, if you will believe God, all things are possible to you. As you now enter into covenant with Him, He will strengthen and keep you and raise you up in power.

If you would like to commit your way to God today and become one with Him in covenant, please pray the following prayer with me now:

Dear God,

I come to You today, in the name which is above every other name, Jesus Christ, the Son of the Living God. Lord, I thank You right now for Your willingness to form, with me, a sacred covenant, an unbreakable and unfailing agreement.

For my part, I agree with You today, by sacred covenant, that from this day forward I will serve You, living for You and worshipping You.

From this day, I will be different. I will be a child of the King and a worshipper of my God.

I repent of every sin and denounce the power of sin in my life.

And today I receive Jesus as my Lord and Savior.

Come into my heart, Lord Jesus.

Take control of my life.

Change me right now.

I surrender my life to You.

I surrender everything to You.

Help me to be faithful to this commitment, as I know You are always faithful to Yours.

In the name of Jesus,
Amen!

Now, friend, just thank and praise God, for He has heard your prayer, and He says to you today: I WILL BLESS THEE. Now go and begin *Discovering the Untapped Power of Covenant.*

A FINAL WORD TO YOU, DEAR READER

It is because of the love of God that reached out to me in covenant that I am able to stand today as a servant of God. Someone loved God enough and loved lost souls enough to come and preach the Gospel, God's offer of this great covenant, to me many years ago, and the result was that I gave my life to Christ the first night I heard that Word preached.

After that, men and women of God loved me enough to take the time and make the effort to nourish and train me, so that today I can stand boldly as a minister of the Gospel. This has all come about because someone cared for me, and if you can show forth the love of God in the same way to others, you will see the same results.

Together, we can change our world, reaching out across the nations and bringing in a spiritual harvest, but it can only happen one lost soul at a time. People will come to know Jesus because of our covenant love.

I love you, dear reader, and it is because of you that this message has now gone forth in print. I know that God has something great in store for you. As you accept His Kingdom love and continue to walk in it, His love working in and through you will cause you to excel in all that you do. Your life will now be joyous, and it will be powerful.

Live in faithfulness to your covenant with God, and He will never fail His promises to you. He says to you today, even as He did to Abraham in days of old: I WILL BLESS YOU.

What we have explored here in the pages of this book is just a beginning. There is so much more in God. His truths are ever fresh and new, and I am still learning new things in Him every day, and I challenge you to do the same.

Continue *Discovering the Untapped Power of Covenant.*

Amen!

Index

MINISTRY PAGE

Apostle David Harewood
Faith City International Ministries
3656 Plank Road
Baton Rouge, Louisiana 70805
Phone (225) 356-1655
FAX (225) 356-1622

www.fcimbr.org
email: davidharewoodministries@gmail.com

www.ingramcontent.com/pod-product-compliance
Lightning Source LLC
LaVergne TN
LVHW011323080426

835513LV00006B/175